Music for Others

Music for Others

Care, Justice, and Relational Ethics in Christian Music

NATHAN MYRICK

OXFORD
UNIVERSITY PRESS

OXFORD
UNIVERSITY PRESS

Oxford University Press is a department of the University of Oxford. It furthers the University's objective of excellence in research, scholarship, and education by publishing worldwide. Oxford is a registered trade mark of Oxford University Press in the UK and certain other countries.

Published in the United States of America by Oxford University Press
198 Madison Avenue, New York, NY 10016, United States of America.

CIP data is on file at the Library of Congress

ISBN 978-0-19-755063-2 (pbk.)
ISBN 978-0-19-755062-5 (hbk.)

DOI: 10.1093/oso/9780197550625.001.0001

1 3 5 7 9 8 6 4 2

Paperback printed by Marquis, Canada
Hardback printed by Bridgeport National Bindery, Inc., United States of America

To Lesley, Ford, and Hasley

Contents

PART II: CARE, JUSTICE, AND BEING FOR OTHERS: A PROPOSAL

Acknowledgments

When one sits down to acknowledge the people who have played a role in the creation of something like a book, it is amazing how long the list of names is. So many incredible people have contributed to this project; they deserve to be acknowledged, and I acknowledge that acknowledging them does not even begin to do them justice. I also acknowledge that I have forgotten to acknowledge far too many, and for that I am deeply sorry.

I must first thank those who participated in my fieldwork, first while I was a doctoral student at Baylor and then afterward as I continued this research. Rev. Dr. Kerry Burkley and the wonderful congregation at Greater Ebenezer Baptist Church were incredible hosts and showed me great hospitality and welcome while I studied with them. Drew Greenway and the congregation of Harris Creek Baptist Church were gracious and insightful. Pastors Kyndall Rothaus and Sharlande Sledge, together with the congregation at Lake Shore Baptist Church, bore my questions and queries with unending grace. Without the participation of these three Christian communities this book would not exist.

The work would also have been incomplete without the assistance of Nate Risdon and Barry Taylor, and their students in Fuller Theological Seminary's *Theology and Popular Music* immersion course at South by Southwest (SXSW) during the spring of 2017. The ability to observe their activities at SXSW and even participate in some of their sessions was an immense boon to my thinking, and their reflections provided needed triangulation for those of the other communities included in this work.

The incredible faculties at Providence University College, Fuller Theological Seminary, and Baylor University deserve more credit than I'm sure I recognize (although any mistakes or infelicities in this text are undoubtedly my own). Karen Sunabacka and the late Henry Schellenberg invested their time and energy in my education—thank you. I'm especially grateful to Jim Bradley, Clay Schmidt, Tommy Givens, Joy Moore, Erin Default-Hunter, Kutter Calloway, the late Glenn Stassen, and Todd Johnson for their investment in my theological education while I was at Fuller and thereafter. Jean Boyd, Alfredo Coleman, Natalie Carnes, and Horace Maxile are exceptional instructors and guides who fielded my inquiries with grace and patience. Elise Edwards gave of her time to lead me in a directed study of feminist ethics. Jonathan Tran guided me through the tangled web of linguistic ethics using Cavell as a road map. Paul Martens listened patiently to my ramblings over lunches, commiserated with me about Prov and metal music, and suffered my half-baked ideas about Christian ethics in the USA. Laurel Zeiss expertly guided me and my colleagues in the initial doctoral cohort of Baylor School of Music through the hoops and red tape that unavoidably accompany a new doctoral degree program.

I owe an extra debt of gratitude to the Church Music faculty at Baylor for their incredible faith and investment in my education. David Music is a legend in his own time, and I am so grateful to have been able to study with him and profit from his wisdom—all the while relishing (and even inciting) his bad jokes. Randall Bradley is the epitome of a tireless leader and scholar, who has faithfully shepherded the Center for Christian Music Studies from its inception to its current height. I will always admire his ability to endure great difficulty with dignity and poise. My advisor, Monique Ingalls, deserves an inordinate amount of credit for her direction of this project during its infancy, from helping to brainstorm the research to proofreading to gently—yet firmly—correcting my errors (and over-caffeinated incidents) and helping me sort out my often jumbled thoughts. She has been the consummate professional who somehow managed to invest in my development as a person at the same time.

I am deeply grateful to the reviewers of this book who offered excellent feedback for improvement. As a scholar, I am buoyed by a sea of peers who are often the inspiration or developers of my best ideas. Lester Ruth, Lim Swee Hong, Timothy Rommen, Jeffers Englhardt, Jeffery Summit, C. Michael Hawn, Birgitta Johnson, and Zoe Sherinian gave their support at various points along the way. Jeremy Begbie has encouraged and supported this project since he sat on my dissertation committee (and passed me, no less!). Sarah Bereza, Josh Busman, Jonathan Dueck, Bo Kyung Blenda Im, Andrew Mall, Maren Haynes Marchesini, Marissa Glynias Moore, Anna Nekola, Adam Perez, Tom Wagner, and Dustin Wiebe have affirmed and challenged me in too many ways to count, and I am grateful to count each of them among my friends. My colleagues at Baylor, Sam Eatherton, Jacob Sensenig, Joe Noelliste, Rob Karns, Maria Montiero, Grant and Leslie Fredrick, Thomas Breedlove, Matt Crawford, James Cochran, Brandon Morgan, Nick Krause, Tyler Davis, and Aaron Houston are incredible humans who willingly engaged with the ideas that resulted in this book while we were students together. Tamisha Tyler has been an incredible colleague since she was my boss in the Fuller Arts Collective. Tanya Riches and Mark Porter read an early draft of this book and gave exceptional and lucid feedback. Melinda Latour pointed out that I was actually talking about care ethics during our walk around Paris in the summer of 2015. Patrick O'Brien has been a faithful friend and spiritual companion since we met in LA in 2011.

Marcell Steuernagel is my great friend and colleague—dudebro! We made it. *Parabéns, idiota!* (Thanks Carol!)

Many friends have inspired much of what is conveyed in this book. Joshua the Bruce has been my best friend since before I was born and undoubtedly inspired my thinking in innumerable ways. John Bottrell has been a creative inspiration and collaborator for almost a decade. John and Jen Warren, CJ and Tami Espinoza, Meg and Andy Stubblefield, and Jenna and Steve Swanson befriended us when we were brand new in Texas. Matt Shantz, Lisa Francis, Jon Grimes, Tyler Stynsberg, Steve Smith, Stephen and Sallie Finkel, Matt Tinken, Jessi and Leland Knippel-Merrit, Rachel Paprocki, Andy Figueroa, and Chris Saunders have inspired me to think and write in new and better ways. Dave Wilmo is a mentor like none other. The Duders (Joe, Johnny, Tim, and Darryl) are more a part of this book than I'm sure I realize.

My early thinking about the intersection of music, faith, and ethics owes a great deal to the members of CTI in the mid to late aughts. Creed, Paulko, Max, Losh (remember that time we almost died in a coup?), C-Bass, JeffHau (one word), Mike Mike, Charger, Kenerly, Aaron, Carl, Carrie, Ed, Eric, Hoagie, and Gretch the Rare Ehret (1983–2015) are incredible humans who have forever changed the way I see the world.

My colleagues at Mercer: Annie Stephens, Katie White, David Keith, Jack Mitchener, Rich Kosowski, Stanley Roberts, and the JFL gang—thank you! My students MaCayla Cook and Benjamin Gessner read an early version of this book for a class and provided valuable feedback.

Finally, my family has been an unfaltering source of confidence and support: Mom, Dad, Anna, Matt, Shane, Shelbi, Bill, Deb, Sam, Grandpa, Grandma, Granny, Tom, Carol, Peg, Paul, Kevin, Rita, Scott, Kay, Leah, Ben, Jon, Naomi, David, Grace, Jimmy, Nina, Little Leah, Mike, Aileen, Grannie, Kenny, and the memories of Granda and Malcolm.

My wife Lesley. Words cannot express my gratitude and love for you. My children, Ford and Hasley—for continually reminding me of what it is to be human.

Introduction

"I'd Rather Not Have It"

In Austin, Texas, during the annual South by South West (SXSW) music, film, and technology conference of 2017, I sat under a tarp in a makeshift seating area near several food trucks. I was speaking with Lacey and Heather,[1] *two twenty-something white women, who were at SXSW with Fuller Theological Seminary's* Theology and Popular Music *immersion course. My reason for being at SXSW was to interview seminary students in a non-liturgical environment concerning the relationship between music's way of being in the world and its way of being in church. In response to my question, "What does music do?", Heather responded, "Music unlocks emotions in me that I didn't even know were possible. It makes me more emotionally intelligent, more emotionally aware of myself, while connecting me to others." Lacey echoed her: "[Music is] an emotional experience. Music is audible emotion. It's people's heart and feelings that you can hear and empathize with." Heather and Lacey went on to extol the virtues of music as being politically important and capable of impelling social change; as contributing to human well-being and human flourishing; as capable of healing. However, the tone of our conversation shifted drastically when I asked them to focus their reflections on congregational music.*

"So . . . what does music do in church?*" I asked, the breeze ruffling the tarp strung overhead. A short silence ensued. "That's a loaded question," Lacey said, frowning, the gravel crunching as she shifted her feet. "I've served on worship teams for years. I feel like worship [is] fakey. We talk about creating these emotional arcs for people . . . and [it] is just manipulative." Heather added, "I've been wrestling with [that] too. I love Hillsong, and they totally do that [referencing the emotional arc]. But, surely God did create the emotions, so surely they do have a role, so I want to have grace."*

Trying to tie these reflections back to their earlier comments about music connecting people in emotionally important ways, I asked "Does music connect people in church?" Lacey's response was ambivalent: she first responded by saying that it does, citing a friend who had lost her faith and still wanted

Music for Others. Nathan Myrick, Oxford University Press (2021). © Oxford University Press.
DOI: 10.1093/oso/9780197550625.003.0001

to sing in church, but then she noted that many churches problematically treat musical worship as a way to disconnect from others, while connecting to God. Heather agreed that congregational music does connect people, but she differed from Lacey in that she felt more connected to others in churches that sang "individualistic" music as opposed to the more liturgical church Lacey now attended. Hoping to get at something that was underlying our conversation, I asked: "Does music in church contribute to your sense of well-being?" Lacey answered definitively, "No. No. In fact, I try to not show up until after the music is over. Even though [the worship leader] is a good friend of mine, and I know her heart, the music is just too much for me. I have such bad memories of it, and I still feel cynical about a lot of it. I'd rather not have it."

Music is an indispensable aspect of human life. It enables human flourishing (Hesmondhalgh 2013), engaging our whole being (DeNora 2011; Higgins 2011 [1991]) while modeling ethical processes for logic and reasoning (Nussbaum 2001). It touches emotions and affections, alerting us to feelings and memories (Turino 2008). It enlivens our senses, creating space for emotion and reason to intersect (Begbie 2011; Meyer 1956). It allows us to encounter others in hospitable (Cobussen and Nielsen 2012), socially constructive ways (Ingalls 2018; Turino 2008; Warren 2014). It affords judgments and evaluations of others (Rommen 2007), and facilitates negotiation of personal and communal values (Porter 2016). Yet it is also capable of inflicting emotional and relational harm, alienating and distorting our perceptions of our selves and others (Hesmondhalgh 2013; Johnson and Cloonan 2008).

Such general descriptions of music's ontology fit equally well into religious contexts. For North American protestants, music is an "indispensable" aspect of public worship in Christian communities (Wren 2000, 43). Indeed, small buckets of ink have been spilled spelling this out. As my interlocutors noted above, and confessional scholars such as Donald Hustad (1993), Harold Best (1993, 2003), J. Nathan Corbitt (1998), Brian Wren (2000), James K. A. Smith (2009), and Jeremy S. Begbie (2011) have similarly noted, music connects people to each other and enlivens our emotional and relational convictions. In Christian communities, these connective and formational properties are imbued with the weight of religious convictions. Such an added layer of significance causes the effects of music's way of being in the world[2] to be more pronounced and to be afforded greater consequence. What are scholars to make of those who are so hurt by the music of Christian communities that they abandon that relational activity altogether, citing manipulation and inauthenticity, thereby negating congregational music's discursive[3] participation in justice?

Music's inherently relational nature strongly suggests that music has ethical significance; if music is so emotionally and relationally powerful, and can be a source of unity and division, then it should be examined from within an ethical frame (Cobussen and Nielsen 2012; Warren 2014). The past two decades have seen something of an explosion of scholarly publications on musical activity and ethics from a wide variety of perspectives. For example, in her landmark mediation on music's ethical importance, *The Music of Our Lives* (1991 [2011]), philosopher Kathleen Marie Higgins offers an extended meditation on the ways that music enriches our lives by virtue of its ability to "enlist the entire 'self'" (xvii). By this she means every aspect of human being: intellectual, emotional, physical, and so on. Building on the work of Peter Kivy and Leonard B. Meyer, among others, she argues that music, with all of its various aspects and expressions, is an ethical model for human life (xx). Building on Higgins' work, Martha Nussbaum highlights the emotional aspects of music to argue for the place of emotion in moral reflection (2001). David Hesmondhalgh's *Why Music Matters* (2013) highlights the relational and social aspects of musical activity and makes a qualified argument for music's contribution to human flourishing.

It is surprising, then, that few scholars of Christian worship have attempted to consider music's way of being in the world from an ethical perspective.[4] On one hand, the work of several praxis-oriented scholars has ethical overtones, but those overtones are not explicitly theorized.[5] On the other hand, several liturgical scholars work on worship and ethics, but completely ignore music—the most widespread participatory activity of Protestant worship—in their analysis.[6] Ethical questions related to music in Christian communities abound when considered through the lens of the brief interview relayed above: How is it that two seminarians can speak so glowingly of music's power for good in general, yet have such strong reservations about music in church? Is there something that confessional scholars are missing in their understanding of music for Christian worship that impels this reaction? Is it possible that the way we treat the activity of musical worship has neglected something vital about its way of being in the world?

These questions point toward what this book argues is a central problem in scholarship on music in Christian worship: that the ethical significance of congregational music has been sidestepped, ignored, or generally undertheorized. Further, failure to pay attention to the ethical dimensions of musical activity in Christian communities has had divisive and destructive results. Complicating matters, earlier scholars of church music have often cast their work in light of many polemic texts surrounding debates about the appropriateness of musical styles for Christian worship without paying more than lip service to the way music functions in people's everyday lives (for example, Johansson 1984, 1992; Lovelace and Rice 1976; Routley 1978; Mitchell 1978; Baker 1985; Frame 1997; Hamilton 1999; Moser 2015). Indeed, such generational conflicts miss the point entirely. An ethical account of music in Christian communities must be able to critically engage affective, relational dimensions of musical activity *before* offering theories about which styles of music ought to be used in Christian rituals.

Unfortunately, the ways that many of these scholars have framed their prescriptions for music have often had unintended destructive consequences; Heather and Lacey's negative reaction to my suggestion that congregational music might have a positive effect on human relationships represents a widely held conception: that even when congregational music *sounds* good, churches *do* music badly. This belief, while lamentable, indicates that congregational music is ethically powerful in ways that transcend stylistic and didactic content, and as such needs examination that pays attention to its relational dimensions.

About This Book

This book is the result of more than fifteen years of practice and research. While it is based on a three-year, multi-site ethnography, the theories I derive from that study are undoubtedly informed by my experiences as a worship leader and touring music minister in over 300 Christian communities across three continents. That final phrase seems as if it should give ample justification for such an undertaking as this, but too often a person engaged in ministry "can't see the forest for the trees," or, in other words, is so consumed by the logistical details of their practice that they are often unable to describe the logic of what they do beyond "best practices." Similarly, a person who tours extensively gets only a snapshot of what life in a given place is like. Yet in both of these capacities I had hundreds of conversations with music ministers and congregants alike who presented me with questions and experiences that demanded more than snapshots of/or best practices—hence, the ethnographic and philosophical research that resulted in this book.

This book is not an *ethnography*, per se, in that it does not seek to describe a place or particular group of people in excruciating detail, but rather it *uses* ethnography to both inform and give evidence of the claims I am making. In so doing, it joins a growing list of books (Scharen 2012; Ward 2012; Ingalls 2018; Lemons 2018; Porter 2020, for instance) that seek to synthesize theory and practice by incorporating ethnographic inquiry with critical theory so as to give a more complete description of what a given activity or event is and means. I have big, theoretical questions that I wish to address, but am wary of theorizing into abstraction.

I also am deeply concerned for the well-being of humanity—especially those who, like me, embrace one of the many Christian traditions. While in a certain sense scholars may stand on the backs of giants, it is important from time to time to step down from those heights and consider what we see at ground level; theories from the backs of giants tend to focus on the peculiarity of the vistas that elevated position affords.

On the one hand, big, abstract, critical theories impel my thinking toward the ground to see what this might look like in everyday life and to find out whether I can identify those theories in the lives of non-scholars. On the other, again and again my experiences in ethnographic fieldwork for this book (and the myriad other musical experiences that impelled that research) inspire and even demand engagement with abstract, critical theories to understand what I have encountered. My task in this book is to stitch together theory and everyday life; to show how and why these big concerns intersect and are interwoven with lived reality in a manner that makes clear how both critical scholarship and human concerns ought to be inseparable.

I assume that if you are reading this book, you have some interest in either music, Christianity, or ethics. Perhaps all three. Standing, as it does, at the intersection of three disciplines, this book is something of a balancing act. By drawing on scholarship from music studies, religious studies/theology, and philosophical ethics, I believe that my argument is thickened and strengthened. Yet I realize that doing so requires me to satisfy the conventions of each discipline without alienating one or the others. Such is the dilemma of interdisciplinary and intersectional scholarship. My solution, such as it is, is to go all the way down with each discipline. Not in a review of literature, of course. Such a book would be profoundly unreadable. Instead, I hope to go all the way down to the core of the disciplinary questions. From a (broadly) musicological perspective, I think through what music is, what it does, what it sounds like, how it is, how people make and encounter it. From a religious studies and theological perspective, I think through how people encounter God and formulate conceptions of ultimacy and meaning in and around musical activity. From philosophical ethics, I think through what it is to be and do good (in terms of both values and virtues), and how "good" is configured in relation to music. Each of these reads and interprets the others.

While I have grand aspirations of offering something that will appeal to the many as well as the few, I realize that such aspirations are seldom realized. Moreover, pursuing such generality inevitably backfires; a book for everyone is a book for no one. So, I have decided to point this book in a specific direction: this is a book about musical ethics in Christian communities. As such, it makes theological and musicological claims. The core musicological claim is that music is inherently relational, and musical ethics must acknowledge and take stock of this reality. The central theological claim is that at its best, Christianity is about just relationships. At its worst, it is about personal power and the ability to control others. Both are encountered in the pages to come.

This book accomplishes two things. First, it demonstrates through ethnographic inquiry and sustained engagement with critical theory how musical meaning and emotion converge in human bodies such that music participates in personal and communal identity construction in affective ways—yet these constructions are not always just. By meaning I mean (pardon the meta-joke) the associations people make between an event or experience and other events and experiences—especially as they pertain to how people understand themselves in relation to others and, in concentric sense, reality. As Marcell Steuernagel has argued, meaning in musical worship is made in a variety of ways, including in response to space (architecture), non-verbal cues, lighting, interior design, and through performance practices (2018, 36, 52–57). However, for many scholars of music in Christian worship—Steuernagel (2018), Porter (2016, 2020), Dueck (2017), Ingalls (2018), and others excepted—"meaning" is most often described in terms of didactic content centered on the lyrics. Indeed, many of my interviewees approached the subject from this perspective as well. Then a funny thing happened. As they told me about their understanding of music in general and congregational music specifically, many began to speak of their experiences as affective and relational—often framing their responses in emotional terms. One pastor even realized this dichotomy during our conversation, and his reflections are explored in greater detail in the final chapter.

Second, it articulates how the ethics of music may best be understood through the lens of "care" with an orientation toward "justice." By care I mean a responsive, reciprocal, and restorative posture toward relationships both near and distant that attentively acknowledges the contributions and capabilities of each as agents within systems of power (Held 1995, 2006; Farley 2002; Nussbaum 2002, 2011; Cannon 2006). Within such a frame, I take relationships to be ontological for human beings—meaning that humans are inherently relational creatures—and demonstrate that relationships are intimately bound up together with affection. If music does, as many scholars suggest and my fieldwork attests, interact with and form emotional postures and affections, then an ethical account of music must consider affect in the context of relationships, and care ethics provides a means of accomplishing this without devolving into a determinative system.

However, while affect, responsibility, and relationships are crucial to how music functions ethically in human experience, when considered in the context of lived reality explored through ethnography, these ideas begin to illuminate how healthy relationships need not only to be caring but also just. Relationships cannot be said to be "good" or "healthy" if they are unjust; affections can be violated by unjust manipulation; responsibilities can be corrupted when uncoupled from orientations toward justice.

Yet justice is not as neat or clean a concept as the preceding lines suggest. Instead, it is contested and debated: justice for whom? Who gets to decide what justice is? What kind of justice should be enacted? Is it just to manipulate emotions and affections for the sake of didactic "truth"? Is it just to violate the ontology of human relationships in retributive ways, or is justice subject to the claims of those relationships? It is here that musical care has something to contribute to the debate: when responsibility and reciprocity are considered within a relational frame, a consideration of justice emerges that is restorative rather than retributive. In this frame, ethical music is music that preserves people in and restores people to just relationships with each other and, as I argue, thereby with God. This relational restoration does not sidestep justice but rather requires it; human relationships are severed by oppression and injustice, so an ethical account of relationships requires an account of justice oriented toward preserving and restoring those relationships, which in turn are only restored when they are just.

Music and Moral Agency

I must mention something here as a way of explaining my understanding of "music": in this book, following Christopher Small (1998), Monique Ingalls (2015), and a host of others, I am considering music as first an activity, then a text (record), of human volition. Christopher Small coined the neologism "musicking" to emphasize music-making as a relational activity and to expand the purview of that activity beyond the creation of sound to any activity related to musical performance (1998). Ingalls (following Small) defines music-making as "the broad range of activities that entails the creation, circulation, and reception of musical sound" (2015, 4), and I am defining it in this way as well. Music can also be understood as a context, a recording, a performance, or a "track" (Zak 2001; Turino 2008; Hesmondhalgh 2013, for example), and examining music as one or all of these will certainly yield fruitful insights.

However, it is as an activity of human volition that can be made to leave a textual record that I consider it here. From an ethical standpoint, music is not a moral agent, that is, it is not responsible for how humans engage with it, although it influences—and perhaps even limits—human agency in important ways.[7] In ethical discourse, an agent is one who is capable of making decisions based on her understanding of right and wrong—values and convictions. Music is not a moral agent because music, that is, the relationally ordered activities and sounds themselves, cannot be held responsible for the effects of their occurrence; you cannot prosecute a harmonic triad or melodic sequence in a court of law in the same way that any other sort of non-human agent cannot be so held accountable.[8] Neither, therefore, can music be considered an "agent" from an ethical perspective, as to do so would be to suggest that the musical sounds themselves may be morally culpable, and therefore regulated (Cobussen and Nielsen 2012; Warren 2014).[9] To give a specific example of how this is so, Wagner's *Der Ring des Nibelungen* is not agentively responsible for how Nazi torturers used it in Dachau;[10] neither is the genre of heavy metal music responsible for its tortuous use by American "interrogators" in Guantanamo Bay (Warren 2014). As is clear from these examples, music is not a *moral agent* because it cannot be proven to be self-generating or directing but rather requires the agency of another for its causality, that is to say, it is not volitional.[11] It is rather the people who employ music in such a destructive manner who are the moral agents (see also Cheng 2020).

In another sense, music may be considered to have a non-human agency (Brabec de Mori 2017; Warren 2021) in that it elicits certain sensations, ideas, and affects among individuals who have been socialized previously to its accepted meanings within a given society (with uncertain and potentially deleterious results, as I argue in the coming pages). But, because I assume that music influences human agency, yet is not a moral agent itself, I treat music as an activity that has formative properties, meaning that its way of being in the world influences human agency and volition by stimulating or perhaps even engendering meaning and emotion within a given context—effects which, in turn, form individuals and relationships while informing musical activities.

Methodology

In order to give both focus and diversity to my argument, I studied three congregations and a para-liturgical focus group in central Texas from 2015 to 2018. Methodologically, my two goals of (1) demonstrating music's meaningfully affective function in constructing and interpreting relational identities and (2) offering an interpretive frame that foregrounds the ethical importance of musical activity are accomplished by applying a triad of research techniques. First, following the contributors to Christian B. Scharen and Aana Marie Vigen's *Ethnography as Christian Theology and Ethics* (2011), Pete Ward's *Perspectives on Ecclesiology and Ethnography* (2012), Christian B. Scharen's *Explorations in Ecclesiology and Ethnography* (2012), and J. Derrick Lemons's *Theologically Engaged Anthropology* (2018), I employed participant/observer ethnography, including interviews, focus groups, and audio and visual documentation, at three churches in the Waco, Texas, area: Lake Shore Baptist Church (Lakeshore), a primarily white, progressive "mainline" style Baptist church with a traditional Baptist music style; Harris Creek Baptist Church, a moderate, suburban, Modern Worship style multi-campus church with multicultural aspirations; and Greater Ebenezer Baptist Church, an urban, African American gospel church with a social justice and holiness tradition.

These three fieldwork sites, described in further detail below, ground my theorizing of music and ethics in lived reality and reveal how music's ethical power is manifest in discrete religious settings. I chose these three churches because each occupied a different stream of evangelical/Baptist tradition and represented something of the diversity of what characterizes evangelical life and polity (Balmer 2006; Mall 2020). Furthermore, each had a musical tradition that was unlike the others, and since musical style and genre is an important aspect of both congregational music scholarship and to the people I interacted with during my fieldwork, placing the perspectives of each into concert with the others yielded insights regarding music's way of being in church that might have been missed if they had not been highlighted by the concerns of one or another tradition.

Additionally, research conducted among Fuller Theological Seminary students at SXSW provides an extra-liturgical perspective, complementing the data gathered by my research in local churches by affording reflection from outside the congregational milieu.

The contribution of ethnography in this project is that it uncovers the gaps between scholarship in the abstract and everyday life. As Christian ethicist Elizabeth Phillips (2012) has argued, theological ethnography is an important means of theorizing effectively, because while doctrines and theories "can be stated propositionally, they must be tested through contact with lived experience" (98). Following Phillips, and the ethnographic turn she describes, I conduct my analysis and draw my conclusions in keeping with her proposed methodology of attentiveness, critical inquiry, and faithful description of what I see and hear. Crucially, my ethnographic research also highlights the differences of musical understanding that exist between church leaders and congregants. It shows that while church leaders speak primarily of church music's significance as one of didacticism and meaning-making, congregants overwhelmingly emphasized music's affective properties as primary. This gap between the musical understanding of "elites" and regular churchgoers was clearly illuminated by my ethnographic work among Fuller Seminary students at SXSW; as seminary students, they occupied a liminal space between congregant and church leader and as such were able to speak of both musical meaning and affect in the same breath.

Second, I engage in close reading of critical theories drawn from a triad of academic disciplines to illuminate music's way of being in the world and the ethical implications of this being: (1) Practical Theology, including theologically informed scholarship on church music and Christian worship, (2) Music Studies, including especially ethnomusicology and the philosophy of music, and (3) Ethics, particularly American Christian and Feminist Ethics. These theories are also used to analyze and interpret my field research findings—even as my fieldwork interrogates these theories: a "transformational" approach to ethnographic and theological analysis (Lemons 2018, 5–8).

Third, continuing in this transformational vein, I employ a constructive methodology to stitch together strands of each in a way that aspires to offer some means of making sense of the ethical impulses experienced by those who engage in musicking. As such, this book gives an account of how the ethical and theological significances of music in Christian communities intersect and merge with each other, demonstrating the ways that relationships are central to both theology and ethics in music.

Fieldwork Sites

It is important to give a detailed description of each site because, despite shared allegiance to a broadly "Baptist" polity ("evangelical" for the paraliturgical site), each had a particular demographic and theological composition. Additionally, my relationship with each fieldwork site differed, and in order to understand both the strengths and limitations of my research, a description of each site together with my relationship to it will illuminate how I analyze my data and draw my conclusions.

Lakeshore Baptist Church

Lakeshore is a congregation of some 500 members formerly affiliated with the Baptist General Convention of Texas (BGCT), and currently affiliated with the Cooperative Baptist Fellowship (CBF) and the Alliance of Baptists, in Waco, Texas (see Figure I.1). The primarily white, middle-class, and highly educated congregation prides itself on being a hospitable and inclusive fellowship. Lakeshore's music may best be described as traditional Baptist congregational singing; that is, it utilized a choir and electric pipe organ (although a piano was sometimes substituted), performed choral introits and Anglican-style anthems, yet drew much of its hymnody from the American folk and white-gospel hymn repertory. Furthering this discursive yet limited mix of musical styles, Lakeshore did not use one of the standard Baptist hymnals but rather used the *Chalice Hymnal* published in 1995 by the Disciples of Christ denomination. The *Chalice Hymnal* is noteworthy in that it has re-texted several common tunes from the folk hymn tradition and updated the language of many classics to be gender inclusive while also eliminating much of the more militant and violent lyrical imagery.[12] Weekly services followed the liturgical calendar and were planned by Pastor Kyndall Rothaus with input from staff, and the four or five songs often aligned with the lectionary and homily for the week.

Figure I.1 Inside Lakeshore's Sanctuary.
Photograph taken by Author, 02/26/2017.

As suggested by Phillips (2012), an ethnographic study of a congregation requires more than just a few snapshots that provide a "theological . . . thick description" (102), but instead requires being involved in the life of the congregation outside of the weekly gatherings. In agreeing with this, I have given Lakeshore a central place in my investigation, because it is the congregation I know best, having been a member there from 2015 to 2019.

Harris Creek Baptist Church

Harris Creek is a mostly white, middle-class congregation that is slightly younger than the congregation of Lakeshore. It has many families with young and teenaged children, and digital technology plays a more prominent role in their musical worship (see Figure I.2). Affiliated with the BGCT, CBF, and Southern Baptist Convention (SBC), Harris Creek had a weekly attendance of around 2,000 persons across four services and two sites. Their main campus, Sunwest, is located off US Highway 84, just outside the Waco suburb of McGregor. The spacious worship center was rapidly becoming too

Figure I.2 Inside Harris Creek's Sunwest Sanctuary.
Photograph taken by Author, 11/05/2017.

small to accommodate their weekly attendance, and during my fieldwork the church had begun constructing a new worship center directly adjacent to their present building. A typical worship service at Sunwest began with three or four songs interspersed with (seemingly) extemporaneous and intercessory prayer. The liturgical calendar was considered, although not explicitly followed to the extent that it was at Lakeshore. Moreover, as one of my interviewees noted, the elements of the Christian year that are embraced by Harris Creek are often unnoticed by the congregation, as they are interwoven with the more typical structure of Modern Worship (Myrick 2018a, 2018c).[13] The musical portion of the worship service was followed by offering and announcements, and eventually by the homily.

Harris Creek's downtown location, the Hippodrome theater and restaurant, follows the same order of service, with both gatherings meeting concurrently. Because of this, while the three or four songs are the same at each site, the musicians differ, so each has its own unique "flavor" from week to week. The sermon from the Sunwest Campus is simulcast at the Downtown campus so that the didactic content does not differ and the meeting times may be consistent at each location.

Greater Ebenezer Baptist Church

Greater Ebenezer is a historic African American Baptist Church most prominently affiliated with the Missionary Baptist General Convention of Texas (see Figure I.3). It is also loosely affiliated with the BGCT. Weekly attendance varies but averaged approximately eighty persons during my fieldwork there. Located in the immediate shadow of I-35, and directly across that thoroughfare from Baylor University's main campus, Ebenezer's is a thoroughly urban church building. It was founded in 1915 on Oak Street as "Oak Street Baptist Church" (some two miles north of the present location) and moved to its

Figure I.3 Inside Greater Ebenezer's Sanctuary.
Photograph taken by Author, 02/04/2018.

current plot in 1925. During the construction of I-35 through Waco (1958–1972), Ebenezer's location was one of contention. During the 1950s, Waco was firmly in the grip of Jim Crow laws, and when the federal government's surveyed route for I-35 through Waco (it was initially planned to circumvent the city) threatened a city landmark, the Earle-Napier-Kinnard House (built in 1858, reportedly the second oldest brick house in Waco), the city council and officials petitioned for a new route. The new route went right through the heart of Waco's thriving African American business district (Gyure 2009). The church was able to remain at its location, but many of the other business and homes were unable to do so. Today, the church is immediately surrounded by construction sites— shopping centers, restaurants, and apartment complexes—that are being built as Waco works to renew its urban core. This renewal is, once again, at the expense of the lower-income families who have occupied the neighborhood on Dutton Avenue where Ebenezer sits, as the ramshackle homes and businesses that surrounded Ebenezer are being demolished in favor of newer Baylor- and Waco-friendly establishments.

As a nod to their heritage, Greater Ebenezer still uses the National Baptist Hymnal (1993), even though it is no longer associated with the conference. Weekly services are highly musical, and song makes up the vast majority of the worship gathering. On a typical Sunday during my fieldwork there, seven or eight songs would be sung, including as a part of the sermon. The single service would begin with a welcome and scripture reading, followed by two or three songs led by the choir or praise team (Ebenezer has three choirs and a youth praise team that rotate Sundays throughout each month, so that nearly every member of the congregation is involved in the musical worship at least once each month, either as a leader or a choir member). This set is followed by a responsive reading, two or three more songs, a benevolence offering, a formal welcome to visitors, another song, the offering and offertory, the sermon (a portion of which is often sung), a call to discipleship, a final song, and a benediction. I asked Pastor Kerry Burkley about the particular musicality of both the service and the sermon, and he said it is a continuance of a tradition from the "plantation" years when "praise and worship would often be used for encouragement and direction as to what to do."

Relationship of Researcher to Fieldwork Sites

My fieldwork positioned me as both an insider and an outsider on several discrete spectrums of identity, revealing how a researcher is eventually often some degree of both in nearly every circumstance. First, I was a member of Lakeshore and served on both the music and finance committees. Additionally, I operated the sound system during the worship services. In this way, I was afforded easy access to pastors and congregants and would consider many of my interlocutors to be friends. This emic position presented both an advantage and a challenge to my ethnography, as some of my conversation partners may have tried to answer my questions based on what they knew of me or my project rather than on what I was actually asking them. As such, I have paid close attention to how I asked my questions and how I coded and analyzed my interviews, being careful to distinguish between accommodation and like-mindedness on the part of my interlocutors. This required seeking clarification at times.

At both Harris Creek and Greater Ebenezer, I was almost a total stranger, although I had a casual relationship with Pastor Kerry Burkley at Greater Ebenezer and worship leader Drew Greenway at Harris Creek. I have also supplied electric guitar at Harris Creek once when Drew was on vacation. It should be noted that, at Greater Ebenezer, my subject position as a white male posed some challenges. I had been asking questions of a predominantly black congregation who has contended mightily against racist gentrification and attempts by developers to "squeeze them out" of their location in what was once the heart of Waco, and I feel a sense of responsibility to do more than simply "not harm"; I do not wish to be yet another white person who wants to take something without giving back. In light of this and other considerations of their social and geographic location, I have endeavored to be extremely sensitive in my research and faithful to offer in this volume something that they may determine is of value.

Finally, as an alumnus of Fuller's master's program who has "gone on" to a career in higher education, I am both an insider (with knowledge of the program and the sorts of questions it generated) and an outsider (I did not know any of the students prior to joining them at SXSW), so I symbolized a unique convergence of knowing and ignorance: in a word, I was "safe."

A final aspect that needs to be addressed is the effect an ethnographer can have on his (or her) fieldwork sites. The impact of my research was especially pronounced at Lakeshore, where I attended and was actively involved in the congregation. After I conducted the first round of interviews with the pastoral staff, I began to be asked to lead in various capacities, first on the music and finance committees, then as the interim chair of the music committee and chair of the search committee for the new director of music, and finally as a deacon. By serving in these capacities I altered the landscape of Lakeshore's music in ways that might not have occurred had I not so served. Yet as Gregory F. Barz and Timothy J. Cooley (2008) point out, there is no way of avoiding this impact. Further still, during his keynote address at the 2017 Annual Meeting of the Society for Ethnomusicology's Southern Plains chapter, Barz argued that ethnographers have an ethical responsibility to advocate on behalf of their conversation partners as they are able: a "response-ability," as he put it. In fieldwork sites where the researcher is an insider, this response-ability can also manifest itself as advocacy and influence in the community itself. Tying back into Barz's and Cooley's initial observations of the unavoidability of one's impact on a research site, it follows that such an impact can be, in a sense, curated through responsive advocacy. Such impact must be disclosed in relating the research findings as a way of mitigating against misrepresented findings, and I do so here in relation to my interviews with several of my interlocutors. On the other hand, after my impact on Lakeshore, as a fieldwork site it seemed to contain too many traces of my activity, and I ceased my research there earlier than at the other two fieldwork sites so as not to inadvertently record too many of my own "shadows" within this writing. Nevertheless, my shadows undoubtedly remain in many ways unobserved by me.

Interview Questions and Processes

In addition to participant observation, my fieldwork is based on interview data collected over the course of interviews with thirty congregants and church leaders from these fieldwork sites. In each interview, I asked the following questions in approximately the same order, although circumstances occasionally dictated an adjustment:

- What does music do?
- How do you experience other people through music?
- Does it make you feel responsible for them?
- Does music do something political?
- Does music influence your sense of well-being?
- Can music heal?
- What makes music "good?"

I then repeated the questions, asking my interlocutors to contextualize their answers with the qualifier, "in church"—for example, "what does music do *in church*?" This second round of questions was often followed by a free-flowing conversation about my work or the subject of my research.

I crafted these questions to relate directly to ethical theories regarding music that have been put forth in recent years. Drawing from Marcel Cobussen and Nanette Nielsen's argument that music's ethical metaphor resides in its hospitable nature, I asked "How do you experience other people through music?" Thinking with Jeff R. Warren's suggestion that music invokes ethical responsibility among its participants, I asked, "Do your experiences of other people in music make you feel responsible for them?" With Timothy Rommen's and Mark Porter's work in mind, I asked, "Does music do something political?" Finally, remembering the work of David Hesmondhalgh and Tia DeNora, I asked, "Does music influence your sense of well-being?" and "Can music heal?" (Rommen 2007; DeNora 2011; Cobussen and Nielsen 2012; Hesmondhalgh 2013; Warren 2014; Porter 2014, 2016).

Since I ground my theoretical reflections in lived reality uncovered by my ethnographic research, I intersperse excerpts from my field notes and interview transcriptions throughout the body of the chapters so as to more clearly show the connections I am making. In keeping with my conviction that my research partners in the field should be afforded qualified equal authority as the scholars I cite and interact with, I have integrated a great deal of my interview data into the body of my chapters. I do this so as not to "exoticize" my interlocutors, "flag up" what is less important, or "virtue signal" my willingness to engage with "normal people." This desire risks paraphrasing or otherwise misinterpreting the words of my interlocutors, of course, and so I have also presented many conversations at length with little or no editing for the purpose of both honoring the thought and words of my interviewees and simultaneously checking my biases.

Organizational Features of the Book

This book is organized into two parts with two chapters in each, not including this Introduction and the Conclusion. The first part examines musical meaning and emotion. It demonstrates that meaning and emotion converge in human bodies in musical activity—especially in Christian communities—such that the inescapable ontology of relationships is unavoidably brought to the fore. The second part takes this fundamental claim as its point of departure and argues that musical ethics must be grounded in this ontology of relationships. As such, the relational ethics of music are bound up together with care oriented toward restorative justice. The first, second, and third chapters are oriented around the major ethical theories I am synthesizing: *discourse*, *formation*, and *care*, with the fourth chapter situating my argument for care and restorative justice in the theological traditions of *response* ethics.

Chapter 1 engages the discursive problem of music in both popular and academic literature, and, using ethnographic evidence gathered from my fieldwork sites, shows that musical meaning is partially determined and simultaneously configured via linguistic and generic means. I suggest that one of the ways communities form is around shared understanding of musical meaning, and that for my interlocutors, musical meaning is determined largely by generic understandings—that musical genres often function discursively for North American evangelicals. Using musical discourse ethics such as Rommen's "ethics of style" and Porter's "cosmopolitanism," I argue that generic musical meaning is imbued with values and convictions, and that these values and convictions are negotiated as a kind of discourse ethics. By applying discourse ethics to the "worship wars," I uncover how the intensity and fervor that characterized these discursive barrages is attributable to the moral meaning ascribed to certain genres and styles by the combatants. However, I further show that these generic understandings of meaning are unstable, being troubled by the competing claims of authenticity and control. This instability precludes ethical theorization on the premise of discourse alone, yet it indicates that the discourse that takes place both around and through musical activity is ethically important and should be taken into consideration in any ethical theory that gives an account of music.

Chapter 2 continues this line of thinking on ethics and music beyond discourse and meaning, and, drawing on ethnographic evidence from Harris Creek and other sites, together with theoretical considerations drawn from the work of Martha Nussbaum (2001), Charles Taylor (2007), James K. A. Smith (2009), Jeremy S. Begbie (2011), and David Hesmondhalgh (2013), argues that the second way that music is ethically significant is through shared experiences of emotional orientation. That is to say that musical activity forms communities through its ability to marshal human emotions and orient emotional postures toward or against ideas or objects. We encounter and experience the emotions and feelings of others in profound ways through music; through contour theory, compound ritual entrainment (CRE), and other ways. These encounters and experiences of others' emotions influence our thinking, and when taken together with the argument of Chapter 1 suggests that musical activity is a site where meaning and emotion intersect. This intersection of meaning and emotion is intensely formational, and my participant-observation at churches along with participants' own descriptions of their experiences reveals how emotion and meaning converge in human bodies. In this way, music forms affective communities, and when we consider that we are formed most profoundly by what we love and desire, it becomes clear that music plays an important role in the formation of both reason and relationships.

Chapter 3 continues this affective, formational trajectory, and, placing the work of Cobussen and Nielsen (2012) into conversation with ethicists such as Martha Nussbaum (2002, 2011) and Virginia Held (2006), argues the specifics of what care will entail in the context of musical activity in Christian communities, both by way of what care ethics addresses and where it may be directed. I couple this interrogation of musical ethics with a concern for restorative justice (Zehr 1990; Braithwaite 2002; Boyes-Watson 2013; Johnstone and Ness 2013) and conclude by weaving together the threads of ethical significance considered here to articulate how the music of Christian communities can respond to the actions and events that those communities encounter.

Chapter 4 picks up on this responsive thread, and, interweaving theological reflections from the traditions of American theological ethics and Jeff R. Warren's (2014) music philosophy with my fieldwork, shows how an ethic of responsiveness makes claims on participants in the activity of musical worship, and argues that caring responsibilities that arise from such musical activity will require attentiveness to both relationships and justice. I further argue that this kind of care oriented toward restorative justice is a Christian response to biblical depictions of "the greatest commandment[s]." I then offer some examples of how this just and caring responsiveness in musical worship may be enacted, concluding with an affirmation of the centrality of relationships for human beings.

A Concern and a Caveat

Understanding music through an ethical frame is not without its challenges. It is useful to point out two hidden dangers in exploring music's ethical significance. First, when music and ethics are considered together, there is often a temptation to identify what music is or is not ethical. I am in no way attempting to determine which musical styles or genres are or are not ethical and therefore appropriate for use in Christian communities, as I argue that, due to the complexity of how musical meaning is created, ethics cannot be evaluated based solely on generic or stylistic criteria. Rather, my approach to identifying ethical music is contextual and situational. I hope to tease out and illuminate salient aspects of musical life that are common to the discrete contexts I am studying in hope that by foregrounding the affective and formational capabilities of musical worship, all musical activity in Christian worship may be practiced in more just and caring ways.

Second, I am not suggesting an ethical system, in the sense that ideas or concepts proceed from one another in a linear fashion. Nor am I creating a constellation of reified ethical principles with which to hold musicking captive. Instead, in accordance with facilitating more just and healthy musical practices, the theories this book develops make clear *how music has ethical power* and *what the results of that ethical power are*. As such, this project is neither purely *prescriptive* nor *descriptive*, but rather *inscriptive*, that is, it is aimed at writing into what is already happening with the intent to clarify and illuminate. This intent does not preclude a thesis, however, and I do argue for a way of understanding Christian musicking's ethical significance such that we may evaluate that activity from an ethical perspective. What my intent does preclude is a step-by-step, "how-to" manual that treats sacred music as a static repertoire and ignores the fact that it can constantly be (re-)contextualized into each new setting that it enters. Instead, I offer a theoretical construction that can be applied with varying amounts of modification to the contexts I study which clarify and offer language for addressing the ethical aspects of music.

PART I

AFFECT, CONNECTION, AND MEANING

Music's Way of Being in the World

1
Discourse
Meaning, Genre, and Cosmopolitan Ethics of Style

Musical Communication and Connection

My first interview at SXSW began during the two-mile morning commute from our billets at Austin Presbyterian Theological Seminary to the Austin Convention Center where many of the keynote sessions were held. As the taxi driver (and owner) of one of the three cars among the Fuller cohort, I was tasked with shuttling students to and from the parking structure at St. David's Episcopal Church, from where they (and I) would walk to the Convention Center. In lieu of monetary payment, the fare for my taxi services was an interview.

My passengers that first morning were three distance education students who had flown to Austin to fulfill the "in person" requirement of the course: Samantha, Ron, and Nick. Samantha, a finance technology manager from Atlanta, Georgia, was the first to respond to my initial query of "what does music do?"

"Oh, interesting. I think it . . . connects."

Ron, a music and arts pastor from Oakland, California, added:

"It unites."

This conviction was expressed by nearly every person I interviewed in my subsequent work among congregations. However, beyond "connection," they had diverse ideas about how that connection occurred and what was important about it. Bev, a choir member at Lakeshore and a librarian, understood this connection to be inspirational and ineffable: "It is where words stop." By contrast, Lakeshore's associate pastor, Sharlande Sledge, noted that music connects people to one another *because* of the words, although she pointed out that this

Music for Others. Nathan Myrick, Oxford University Press (2021). © Oxford University Press.
DOI: 10.1093/oso/9780197550625.003.0002

connection was not entirely cognitive: "The words are very important. . . . [The] main role of music in the church is that it is something that people can do together. . . . [I]n congregational music we all sing together. So, we are singing words of faith that we [may] not understand at the time." Others, such as Heather and Lacey, the two Fuller students discussed in the Introduction (and later in this chapter), noted that music connected people emotionally:

> H: I think, for me, when I hear music it unlocks emotions in me that I didn't even know [were] possible. . . . I think music makes me more emotionally aware. And maybe even . . . "emotionally intelligent." I think it . . . makes me more emotionally aware of myself, but it also connects me with other people.
>
> L: [Music is] an emotional experience. Music is audible emotion. It's people's heart and feelings that you can hear. And empathize with.

Still others, such as Stan, an English professor and member of Lakeshore, noted the expressive nature of musical connection: "I think that it allow[s] people . . . to express themselves as individuals [that] are part of the collective."

These brief examples illuminate the diverse, complex, and profound ways that music connects people. The essence of these reflections may be summed up singularly as "communication":[1] music connects through expressing "inspirational, ineffable" thoughts and "emotions" through words and sounds that are "audible" and able to be "empathize[d] with." This synthetic statement represents (if only in part) the diversity and complexity of how human beings experience the communicative power of music while underscoring the commonalities. While topics such as "emotional intelligence" and "ineffability" will be picked up in subsequent chapters, examining the many ways that music communicates provides both a frame and lens through which to understand music's connective way of being in the world. Further, as the preceding excerpts demonstrate, communication is *one of the most obvious ways that music connects people and builds communities.* Yet communication-cum-community formation is not always a definable "good"; sometimes those communities are formed in opposition to other such communities—to destructive effect.

Discourse Ethics and Music

A helpful way of identifying the root of these concerns and responding to them is known as *discourse ethics.* Discourse ethics is concerned with providing and protecting acceptable means of declaring personal conviction, values, and identity. It is furthermore concerned with establishing the criteria of flourishing, and the means by which the people most directly affected by the topic of deliberation thereby negotiate the power to say how they understand themselves to flourish. Bound up in what Charles Taylor describes as the ethics of authenticity (1992), discourse ethics is concerned with the ability to declare your convictions and values, putting those expressed needs into conversation with the needs of others and thereby negotiating differences and similarities while preserving the right of each as individuals (see Habermas 1990 for more).[2] Further, these declarations of values, convictions, and identity are vital for communities to form and flourish, as truthful declarations provide the materials for honest consensus between individuals (see Rawls 1999).[3] How, then, does music participate in such ethics?

Timothy Rommen, in *Mek Some Noise: Gospel Music and the Ethics of Style in Trinidad* (2007), draws heavily on the work of Jürgen Habermas to argue that musical style has discursive characteristics, although Rommen notes that Habermas does not offer a "theoretical model to which I am unequivocally drawn or which I can use in an uncomplicated way" (30). He notes that while Habermas "attempts to ground discourse ethics in a carefully argued and universalist approach to justice, his model itself is predicated on a procedural approach to consensus through communicative action whose susceptibility to the individual, personal, ethical thought-life of subjects is illustrated in the very ambiguity that often surrounds attempts at moral discourse" (32). Rommen sees in this gap the space for music's discursive function to flourish, albeit in ways that interrupt the flow of Habermasian discourse ethics (34–36).

Building an argument in this discursive gap, Rommen argues that musical styles function discursively for the communities he studied in Trinidad. In the same way that certain words and combinations thereof provide the raw materials for discourse ethics to function, so the certain combinations of sounds we call "styles" and "genres" provide the means by which certain ethical evaluations are made.

Yet this argument is not universal. Mark Porter's *Contemporary Worship Music and Everyday Musical Lives* (2016) continues Rommen's methodological approach and similarly builds on the foundation (cracks and all) that Habermas and Rawls laid. Yet while Porter affirms Rommen's thesis of an ethics of style in certain contexts, he notes that the values and convictions associated with certain styles of music in the everyday lives of his conversation partners were not necessarily the same as those within the music with which they worshipped in church, and in large part they did not perceive the difference as presenting a problem. Instead of reinforcing the "sacred/secular divide," such "musical cosmopolitanism" afforded hospitable and charitable negotiations of individual identities and ethics while simultaneously allowing for those values and ethics to be expanded and enlarged (50–52, 153–154).[4]

That congregational music has a discursive ethical dimension should come as no surprise to music scholars; however, few have endeavored to examine and theorize about its significance. As suggested by Porter, discourse ethics provides a helpful paradigm for evaluating the negotiation of both ethical values and ethical identities (2016, 152). When Christians sing together they proclaim their beliefs and values, embodying with their voices the perspectives of good belief and practice conveyed by the musical texts (subject to certain qualified criteria, see Engelhardt 2015). Discourse, then, is an apt paradigm with which to begin constructing an ethics of congregational song.

As many scholars have noted, music is *not* a universal *language*. Moreover, as Aaron Fox and Steven Feld have argued, music is inherently different from language, in that it serves a different purpose and utilizes different conventions—despite sharing a common physical dimension (1994, 1999). How, then, can discourse ethics uncover something of music's ethical significance? The answer to this question is bound up in a range of intersecting strands of human activity, and it is to the first of these strands, the conventions of musical genre, that I now turn.

Musical Genre and the Discursive Construction of Musical Meaning

Although musical genre is complex and contested, it is still a useful starting point for this discussion of meaning in musical discourse, as it frames the ways that people talk about music, choose to participate in musical activity, and make early evaluations of others. Indeed, it is almost a truism that different genres communicate different values and convictions. Many people, such as Joan, the head usher at Lakeshore, ascertain what musical genres their friends like in order to determine what their values and convictions are and thereby negotiate relationships:

> I have friends that listen [to all kinds of music]. Some of them are I would say '50s, '60s '70s listening to classical, calming music, whereas I have friends that listen to punk rock. Some listen to Rock n' Roll, some listen to progressive country, some listen to what I consider the twangy-type country, and I have a few that actually listen to this acid rock head-banging stuff . . . [knowing this is how] you learn about them . . . what they like . . . whether they're introverted or extroverted [etc].

Her reflections, coupled with those of many others, indicate that people understand and take advantage of the fact that musical meaning is generically and relationally constructed, both in how meaning is established and how relationships are experienced in light of that construction.

As Simon Frith argues (1996), a musical genre's meaning and the verbal discourse surrounding that genre are co-constitutive. As such, musical genres are an important way that people both identify and negotiate moral and ethical issues in Christian communities; indeed, both Rommen and Porter connect musical style and genre to discourse ethics directly.

Broadly, musical genres establish a categorical methodology by which musical meaning can be triangulated, both sonically and socially (Fabbri 1982; Frith 1989, 1996; Cook 1998; Moore 2001; Holt 2007). Genres provide rules that govern a given music's participation in that mode of meaning-making. Allan F. Moore argues that genre and style are different from each other yet are related in "orthogonal" ways, meaning that they intersect in a manner similar to matrices (2001). Moore further argues that generic categories provide the context through which musical gestures make meaning: "style refers to the manner of articulation of musical gestures and is best considered as imposed on them, rather than intrinsic to them. Genre refers to the identity and the context of those gestures" (2001, 441).

This is to say that within the configuring limits of a genre, the style of the music performed—that is, the concrete elements of notes, chords, tempi, timbre, rhythm, and so on—contribute to the configuration of meaning in relationship to the socially accepted values of the genre, although thinking with Moore I agree that these are not "nested" terms and concepts. For example, in the genre of Western art music at the turn of the twentieth century, the compositions of Claude Debussy were rightly understood to be a critique of the Romantic values inherent in the genre at that time (Auner 2013), though they are now categorized within Romanticism. To offer a more prescient yet hypothetical example, a worship band performing hymns in the style of punk rock in a congregation that valued traditional piano and organ accompaniment and simply sung American folk tunes would be understood as performing a critique—and possibly a violation—of the values espoused by that congregation, whereas performance adhering to the established style of the genre (of traditional instrumentation and folk tunes performed in an unadorned manner) would be understood to support those values.

This way of thinking about musical genre communicating values and convictions is helpfully demonstrated by many of my interviewees. Later in my interview with Samantha, Ron, and Nick (the three Fuller students introduced earlier) during our commute to the Austin Convention Center at SXSW, our conversation turned to music in church and worship. Their reflections illustrate how genre and style may communicate in ecclesial settings and begin to uncover something of the ethical importance of generic communication.

> S: You know [music is] powerful, or it can be something that is so bad or so foreign to them that it distracts them from the greater purpose. So, my church is a bunch of old white people . . . [laughter]. . . . [I]t's an Anglican church, if I were to go in, and do a rap song . . .
>
> N: Oh, please invite me!
>
> S: . . . It wouldn't be good for them, because they're just gonna get irritated. And the end goal is for them to be able to assent and to commune, and that is not where they're at. And so I think in terms of curating music it's important.
>
> R: That's your responsibility as the curator, but if I go to your congregation, I prolly wouldn't feel any responsibility to those people. I would in *mine*, singing with people I'm gonna see next week, and the next week after that.
>
> N: But there is some sense of communal aspect through the music. I dunno if I feel it, but I mean, church services historically were designed that way; there's a reason that churches follow a lectionary, so that churches all over the map are one in spirit at the same time, or roughly the same time each day. We're reading the same prayers or singing the same songs; even though we're separated by miles and miles and miles, we are one.

As the group's comments reveal, the values and convictions communicated by musical style and genre depend in large part on the meaning attributed to them by the community—sometimes over and against another such community. As Samantha's remarks indicate, her "old, white" Anglican congregation in Atlanta, Georgia, would feel that their trust in her as a worship leader was violated if she were to perform a hip-hop song during morning worship because of the convictions and values that hip-hop represents to them. Thus, performing hip-hop would constitute a violation of her responsibility to them (the theme of responsibility generated by music will be examined further in Chapter 4). However, as Ron's comments indicate, there are limits to the ethical responsibility congregations can impose on their leaders (and vice versa): as a visiting artist or leader, this person would have no obligation to maintain stylistic trust in that way and would therefore be free to perform a hip-hop song in Samantha's congregation (although if Samantha invited him she may face criticism). In view of the power dynamics Samantha mentioned, Ron's comment implied that as a leader coming into a congregation from outside, he would have greater freedom to confront systemic racial injustice that the values and convictions of the genre of hip-hop confronts (see Todd Boyd 2003, 2007).[5]

Nick's final comment draws out some of what informs the ethical dilemma surrounding musical genre and style in worship: Do the commitments of a leader to a specific community dictate the terms of that leader's ethical responsibility to them, or are Christians held to a broader standard of ethical responsibility as being of a single, diverse community of faith that makes claims upon their allegiances—sometimes in spite of their commitments to a certain ethnic or economic community? Stated differently, an underlying concern for all three was whether it would be "good" for the congregation to disrupt their patterns of worship with a musical genre that they understood as opposing the values of the majority of the congregation. In this particular example, the question of generic disruption is framed as an issue of generation and race: Samantha's is an "old, white" congregation. As Emilie Townes observes, whiteness carries with it connotations of power, privilege, and systemic control (2006, 109); therefore, would it necessarily constitute an ethical act if a "white" congregation were confronted with the critique that would be offered by rap music? I will let these questions hang for the moment (although they will be further explored in the coming chapters) as my purpose in asking them is to draw out both the ethical significance of musical style and genre *and* to interrogate the value of such discourse for ethical deliberation, the second of which is the focus of this chapter.

The Ethics of Genre and Style

I sat in Alpha Omega, a small Greek restaurant in Waco, Texas, with Bob, a white male in his mid-forties who attended Lakeshore and sang in the choir, serving as interim choir director at various times. Bob had been at Lakeshore for thirteen years and was well acquainted with the community's musical life. Our conversation about music's way of being in the world focused on Lakeshore's values of hospitality and inclusiveness, and I asked Bob how he thought Lakeshore's music reflected those values.

> B: I can give you a mixed answer. In terms of being sensitive to gender and other kinds of social issues, the music at Lakeshore really excels at that. On the other hand, the fact that Lakeshore has a tradition of using Western art or high church music or what have you, depending on your perspective, that could be seen as not as inclusive. I know that we have tried at various times to incorporate other types of music. We do have a lot of old traditions mixed in with more traditional Western art type worship music. But I know that with the nature of our church, with lots of people that are highly educated, that the music overall, I think, tends to reflect the "typical tastes," if you will, of those people.

Bob's reflections reveal how musical style and taste are almost inextricably associated with certain socioeconomic class status; his linking more traditional styles of music to "highly educated" people's tastes is a common refrain for many. I asked Bob whether he thought musical style communicates different things to different people, and he responded by telling a story of a friend who had moved away before I came to Lakeshore:

> B: He had been away from the church for forty years before he came to visit Lakeshore and came along with some relatives. When he first came, he had a negative experience—he eventually joined but had a negative experience at first because *they played a hymn tune that he recalled from his childhood that brought back a lot of negative memories.*

Bob's reflections indicate that musical style has profound discursive power in part because it is fundamentally tied to social identities (such as socioeconomic class) and to personal memories. Rommen articulates the discursive function of certain styles within the overarching genre of Trinidadian gospel music and the ethical perspectives demonstrated thereby that illuminate Bob's reflections. As I noted earlier, Rommen suggests that certain styles of gospel music (such as Gospelypso) are rendered problematic not necessarily because of aesthetic, political, or even commercial interests but because of what he calls the "poetics of conviction," the associations made between real beliefs and musical activities (2007, 27–28). Rommen establishes this claim by observing that ethical considerations are established before aesthetic considerations. For example, the lifestyle associated with the musical style of calypso music by some of Rommen's interlocutors is one of sensuality and debauchery; Gospelypso, as a Christianized version of calypso, sonically represented those same values to some church leaders. For those leaders, the lifestyle associated with what the music sounds like matters more than how the performers actually live. In this way, the actual lifestyle of the performer of the music is secondary to the lifestyle associated with the musical style (Rommen's interlocutors comprise both sides of this debate, and he does not argue for the merit of either but rather demonstrates that musical style is ethically significant for what it represents to the listeners). This seeming contradiction is resolved by an ethical valuation of truthfulness; if you are performing the style of music associated with immoral living while living morally yourself, you are being untruthful through your performance.[6] While being careful to avoid an ethics of utility, Rommen posits that (in the context of Full Gospel Churches in Trinidad) "musical style is being put to use in order to achieve certain goals . . . that are informed by personal convictions" (2007, 28–29, 35).

Bob's friend had an adverse reaction to the style of Lakeshore's music because of the convictions he associated with it due to his previous experience in Southern Baptist churches. However, that Bob's friend eventually joined the church indicates that the discursive value of musical genre was not the final word on the matter for him (as Porter suggests)—although it can be for others.

One such example is CJ, a white male in his mid-thirties who attended Harris Creek and whom I interviewed during my fieldwork there. CJ and his family visited Lakeshore, and while they appreciated the teaching, community, and theological position of the church, they ultimately decided that they could not worship there due to the style of music performed in the church. They had moved to Waco the previous year for work and had done some of the proverbial "church shopping"—which he lamented, as he believed it demonstrated a lack of commitment on his part—on their arrival. I knew from a previous conversation that they had visited Lakeshore but ultimately chose to worship elsewhere, so I asked CJ what went into that decision for him.

> CJ: I didn't grow up [going to] church. The first church that I went to didn't sing hymns—it wasn't until I went to [college] after high school [that I] first experienced hymns. And it was crazy because other people [grew up singing] hymns and everything; they had their favorites, and I'm like, "I have no idea what we're singing." So [Lakeshore's music] was just different than [what I'm familiar with]. I get it, but it's harder for me to connect to. It takes more effort to do that. It's not natural for me. . . . Harris Creek is definitely more contemporary; it's more like a three- or four-piece band, a couple of people singing, it's more—I don't want to say "relevant," but just more recent music. So [I'm] coming from a different kind of tradition and [Harris Creek has] more contemporary versions of music. It's less about quality and more about just comfort. Being able to connect.
>
> Author: Does that style of music that Lakeshore does communicate something to you? Does that represent something either historically in your life or just sort of something that you think of in society?
>
> CJ: I think it's really, well, yeah—it does communicate something. I think the thing that it communicates to me is, well, it let me know that I'm in Texas; that I'm in the Bible Belt. I'm from the left coast or the West Coast. So, it communicates to me that and it feels—it was confusing. You had this traditional way of worship. But then there was a woman who's a pastor, which I think is awesome, but it just is like "Wait, what?" OK, so we're still here in this way (music), we're so progressive in this way (female pastor), I was like, "I don't understand. I like this part, and it's not that I don't like this, but . . ." If my family had been onboard I'd be like, "OK I can make this work. It's not like I can't make this work." But, it communicated that [traditional "church" music] . . . I think it communicates the age of the church, I think [it] communicates the priorities of the church, and it's not necessarily positive or negative but I think it communicates that these are the people, this is where we're at right now. So, we're going to keep [doing] church this way because this is what is comfortable for the people that are here.

CJ's perspective offers crucial insight into the diversity of generic discourses in church music and suggests that such generic discourse may be insufficient for determining values and convictions. CJ's reflections on his experience of visiting Lakeshore highlight several important facets of musical genre's discursive function in churches. First, and importantly, what is communicated by musical genre depends in large part on the experiences of those who encounter it and the context in which it is encountered; for CJ, the performance of "traditional" hymns to piano and organ accompaniment at Lakeshore "let me know I was in Texas; in the Bible Belt." This communicative function, for CJ, was based on his experience growing up unchurched on the West Coast, and then on his experience of church there after converting to Christianity. Second, the music at Lakeshore communicated traditional values and convictions that emphasized his position as an outsider; implicit in his recognition of "Texas, the Bible Belt" is an idea of exclusivity, of feeling unwelcome. On the contrary, he found that contemporary pop-rock–based music at Harris Creek conveyed comfort and gave him the "ability to connect." Third, though he was put off by Lakeshore's "traditional" music, his interpretation of Lakeshore as a whole as "traditional" was troubled by the church's "progressive" theology and politics, with which he was comfortable; he struggled to make sense of the apparent juxtaposition that traditional church music *and* progressive theology presented to him.

As Porter helpfully observes, ethical values and convictions do not remain static in relation to the music of Christian communities but are rather actively negotiated there through ongoing discourse (2016). This negotiation does, I think, constitute something of a formation as it follows that formation occurs in a progressive manner through ongoing negotiations of meaning and experience. Porter's point, however, serves to fill in and illuminate the complex—and important—relationship between personal and communal convictions as demonstrated musically. CJ's interpretation of what the music at Lakeshore communicated about its convictions and values may surprise many among that congregation, as Bob's comments suggest. Indeed, among Lakeshore's key values are hospitality and inclusiveness, which is the opposite of how CJ and his family interpreted Lakeshore's music. However, further conversations among current members revealed that Lakeshore's musical practices are interpreted very differently by many of its congregants as well. Exploration of this difference reveals how musical genres are constructed using non-musical elements together with musical ones; how genres communicate—and at times fail to communicate—values and convictions, and how this variance of meaning both necessitates and challenges ethical evaluation.

Generic Conflicts and Stylistic Battles: The "Worship Wars"

The diversity of ways that musical style may be interpreted is tragically demonstrated by what has become known as "the worship wars" in North America. The worship wars were a series of ecclesiological disputes over musical style, genre, and instrumentation that transpired among evangelical and some mainline protestant churches during the 1990s and 2000s (Nekola 2009, 2016; Justice 2012, 2017; Lim and Ruth 2017; Ruth 2017a, 2017b; Ingalls 2018). Anna Nekola notes that the term may have been coined in Lutheran theologian Ted Peters's article "Worship Wars" (1994), noting that Peters's article connected conflicts over musical style in worship to the "culture wars" of the 1970s and '80s; terminologically it may have helped to associate the debates over music with the gravitas of warfare (Nekola 2009, 105). Nekola further states that the conflicts were also over understandings of ecclesial purpose: Were evangelical churches an evangelistic institution or were they discipleship oriented (2009, 1)? Deborah Justice (2017) agrees and argues that the conflicts were also indicative of social-economic differences that were latent in the combative churches. Terry York (2003) adds to this description by drawing attention to the generational and theological differences that also contributed to the conflict while arguing for a cessation of hostilities.

While each of these accounts of the motivations behind the worship wars is surely correct in degrees, each acknowledges that on the surface the conflicts were over what certain combinations of relational musical sounds meant. Some who opposed "praise choruses" (what came to be called "Contemporary Worship Music"), such as Calvin Johansson (1992), saw in them the advance of secularism into the church. Others, such as John Frame (1997), saw contemporary worship music as symbolically breaking churches free from their old legalism and irrelevance. Others, such as Marva Dawn (1995), were more charitable toward the other side of the conflict. However, the ongoing effects of the worship wars are such that musical style matters in churches, and it matters ethically for many people. How did musical style come to be so morally imbued? What lies behind the associations that these various styles took on, and what might an understanding of those associations reveal?

We can begin to answer these questions by examining an experience I had at Lakeshore when I was beginning my fieldwork there. For Lakeshore's members, the musical styles that were the subject of the worship wars—"traditional" hymnody that espoused a Western art music aesthetic versus "praise choruses" that followed the conventions of pop and rock music—were connected with theological and ethical values. Further, discourse about these values gave rise to divisions over the use of extra-musical material objects (such as digital projectors) that could potentially facilitate "the wrong kind" of musical activity.

Fieldnotes: November 18, 2015, Waco, Texas. *My first business meeting after joining Lakeshore Baptist Church was held after the Wednesday evening meal and prayer service. The topic for discussion was a vote on whether to purchase a projector and screen for the church. The proposal had been brought forward by the associate pastor, Sharlande Sledge, and had been taken up by Sam, a middle-aged congregant who was an economics professor.*

"I'm just afraid that if we get a projector and a screen it will be a slippery slope, and eventually we'll have drums and guitars and start singing praise choruses," an elderly congregant said into the microphone. Sam responded, "We wouldn't use it for music or worship but would use it for pictures and presentations. Remember how John's[7] *family wanted to have a photographic slide show at his funeral? This would allow us to do that." His attestation that the projector would not be used to show lyrics on the wall failed to convince those opposed to the idea. Sam and others in favor of the projector confirmed that they did not want to have "praise choruses" for worship and that the projector was merely a tool to enhance the life of the church—but to no avail. The discussion was tense from the beginning, and it was obvious that the projector was a highly contentious issue. One congregant loudly voiced her opposition to the motion in no uncertain terms using language that can only be described as colorful. Others, too, were strongly opposed to the measure, citing fears that it would ruin the aesthetics of the sanctuary, distract from worship, or be a misallocation of funds.*

The "younger" people (thirties and forties) I sat with during the discussion were equally amused and exasperated by the proceedings; at one point, after a dubious member had continually stated that she just could not picture how the projector and screen would look in the sanctuary, someone remarked—under their breath but loud enough to be heard—"If we had a projector I could show you." In the end, after some two hours of back and forth discussion, the vote went overwhelmingly against the projector, despite broad agreement among the elderly congregants that a projector would be nice for funerals.

Why did a Baptist church of Lakeshore's general description (see Introduction) so vehemently oppose the purchase of a projector and screen? It was evident from the discussion that the projector itself was not the root of the opposition as the majority agreed it would be a useful tool; rather, it was the association of the projector with "praise choruses" and contemporary worship music, coupled with the belief that a projector's purchase represented a "slippery slope" toward musical change. Why, then, was the congregation at Lakeshore so opposed to "praise choruses," to the point that it refused to buy a multi-functional piece of technology because it could facilitate the performance of this type of music?

The answer to that question can be found in how the meaning of musical genre is bound up with both the history of Lakeshore and its relationships to the Southern Baptist Convention. During the 1980s and 1990s, the SBC experienced what is known either as the "conservative resurgence" or the "fundamentalist takeover," depending on the perspective of the one speaking (Hefley 1991; James et al. 1999), when the leadership of the denomination began pursuing a more explicitly right-wing agenda. Lakeshore's congregants overwhelmingly consider the event the "fundamentalist takeover," and stories abound of the leadership of the church "contending against the fundamentalists" during the SBC meetings of the 1980s and '90s. Lakeshore formally left the SBC in 2000 when it became clear to them that the "fundamentalists" had indeed taken over.

Interestingly, during the time of my research, the style of music used within worship was one of the most prominent reminders of Lakeshore's painful break with the SBC. To Lakeshore's congregants, "praise choruses," or as liturgical historians Swee Hong Lim and Lester Ruth call them, contemporary worship songs (2017), have come to symbolize "fundamentalism." Just as Lakeshore broke with the SBC, so also did it attempt to expunge any music it felt smacked of fundamentalism. For Lakeshore, moving away from the SBC necessitated a rejection of contemporary worship music. Pastor Sharlande Sledge explained it like this:

> Some twenty years ago we switched from the Baptist hymnal. . . . We did a big study of what we were singing and what we were doing in worship, and we had been copying hymns from the book of hymns by Jane Parker Huber. . . . We ended up with *The Chalice* hymnal, which is the Disciples of Christ['s hymnal]. [We weren't moving] towards the Disciples of Christ; we were getting involved in the Alliance of Baptists and the Cooperative

Baptist Fellowship, *moving away from all things SBC*, but trying to stay Baptist.

Perusing SBC hymnals since the split seems to confirm Pastor Sledge's explanation. Since Lakeshore left the denomination, the SBC's hymnal offerings have included an increasing number of songs considered "praise choruses" by Lakeshore's congregants: contemporary worship songs make up no fewer than 189 of the 271 hymns in the *2008 Baptist Hymnal* absent from the SBC's last hymnal offering before the resurgence/takeover, the *1991 Baptist Hymnal*.[8]

While the *2008* was published some ten years after Lakeshore adopted *The Chalice*, Lifeway, the publishing wing of the SBC that produced the *2008*, did not compile the hymnal by assembling a committee of scholars and pastors to determine which songs should go in the hymnal; rather, it developed a market research division, Lifeway Research, to determine which songs were the most appealing to certain age groups (Fultz 2010). Daniel D. Fultz, in his 2010 dissertation "Style Matters: Worship Preferences of University Students Regarding the Use of Music and Technology," noted that during the process of developing the *2008* hymnal, Lifeway Research published a series of articles claiming that while 70 percent of sixteen-year-olds attend worship services at least twice a month, only 31 percent of nineteen-year-olds do so. While the percentage of churchgoers recovered slightly as respondents aged, the conclusion drawn by Lifeway Research was that young people were leaving the church and, for the most part, were not returning (Fultz 2010, 10). As Fultz notes, Lifeway and other similar denominationally affiliated businesses accepted (or indeed, developed) the idea that musical style was an important means of retaining their members (2010, 11–13); it was this impulse that led Lifeway to place such high emphasis on contemporary worship songs in the *2008* hymnal,[9] as those were the songs that young people were listening to and enjoying as evidenced by their popularity and commercial success (Ingalls 2018). The reasons for this connection are twofold: first, as Fultz's work argues, people who use digital technology more in their daily lives are more apt to appreciate its use in worship, and second, the people who use digital technology more in their daily lives are primarily younger (2010, 93). As contemporary worship music is by and large a technologically driven activity in ways that extend beyond the boundaries of the "technology" of hymnals, organs/pianos, and voices, it follows that younger people who appreciate the increased access to congregational music that newer technologies afford will be more appreciative of newer musical offerings (interestingly, Fultz states that the use of electronic technology such as a projector is associated with contemporary worship music across much of the Midwestern United States [2010, 10], perhaps revealing some of the reasons for Lakeshore's reticence to acquire one).[10]

As Philip V. Bohlman writes, "Music accumulates its identities . . . from the way it participates in other activities" (2000, 288–289). For Lakeshore's congregants, the SBC's move toward fundamentalism is symbolically represented by the SBC's concurrent embrace of contemporary worship music, and subsequently contemporary worship music symbolizes the SBC's turn toward fundamentalism to Lakeshore's congregants. However, for CJ and others, Lakeshore's musical genre communicated values of exclusion and out of touch traditions commonly associated with stuffy, dogmatic churches (later in our conversation, CJ and I noted how the genre of music at Lakeshore is often used in films to represent churches with backward ways of thinking). Yet Lakeshore's pastors and many of its congregants understand the values and convictions communicated by their musical genre as being progressive and inclusive; antithetical to their perception of SBC fundamentalism. These competing understandings of a musical genre's discursive properties begin to illustrate how musical meaning, and subsequent ethical discourse, is often understood in very different ways.

Music and Language: Different in the Same Kinds of Ways

Part of what makes the application of discourse ethics to musical activities so difficult is the tantalizing similarity yet profound and even irreconcilable differences between music and language (and I am thinking here about Western languages such as English, German, Spanish, and French, in particular). As Steven Feld and Aaron Fox have observed, music is "typically, syntactically far more redundant and overdetermined yet semantically far more diffuse and underdetermined than language" (1999, 159). Nonetheless, Feld and Fox conclude that music and language share common communicative worlds (162). A key feature of these shared worlds is the voice as a "representational trope for social position and power" (1994, 26). The challenge to evaluating musical communication within a discursive ethical frame is that, as noted above, music and language do not share the same methods of determining meaning: How can you determine the ethical merit of a music if you do not know what it means and therefore what it does? Furthermore, as Anna Nekola has noted, music's communicative, that is, discursive activities are often unnoticed (2015, 2). Nekola argues that applying communication paradigms to music is tricky, as music does not transfer meanings in a one-to-one fashion but rather mediates between ideas, concepts, and people in various and sometimes contradictory ways. Indeed, she argues that the use of a "transmission model" of language in music is ill-advised as music does not, in actuality, "transmit" discrete messages that have only one meaning. She helpfully summarizes the transmission model as having a problematic tendency to "focus on communication as a direct process of information encoded by a source and sent to a receiver to be decoded" (2015, 8). Instead, Nekola argues that meaning and messages are "mediated" in multilocutionary forms: through words that afford certain meanings, through gestures that determine the apparent meaning of those words for listeners and congregants, through the type of audio or visual media used to present lyrics or amplify sound, through locally inflected musical stylings that situate the meaning of the music and lyrics relationally to one another and the specific congregation in question. This reality has ethical implications for how people engage and understand music's communicative (that is, mediating) power in Christian settings.

Musical meaning lies at the heart of music's discursive function in lived reality. As Porter points out, much recent scholarship in musicology and ethnomusicology has shifted the locus of emphasis on how musical activities make meaning away from notions of "absolute music" and toward the diverse ways that *all* music makes meaning and how that meaning is socially constructed (2016, 32; cf. Meyer 1956, 33–38). However, scholars working on church music still differ in how they treat the communicative function of music. Christian worship scholars such as Debra and Ron Rienstra, for instance, employ a transmission paradigm to understand how music communicates, assuming that words have established meanings and reliably communicate the intention of the speaker to the listener (2009, 36). Focusing on the lyrics of congregational songs as the primary means by which a message is transmitted and a community is formed, they argue that great care and attentiveness to the words of the song as well as the words chosen to direct the congregation need to be exercised to form authentic Christian communities (36–53).

Other musicologists, such as Allan F. Moore, suggest that music within Christian worship communicates in diverse ways that are not always determined or reliable. Giving an account of how singing and speaking are two different locutionary functions, Moore examines how the performative actions of the worship leader further affect the meaning of the words, and how music might play a role in determining those actions (2015, 185). In contrast to Rienstra and Rienstra's suggestion that "[worship] words are performative; as we speak them, we are doing what we say" (2009, 44), Moore argues that the words themselves are only one aspect of the communicative function of music in Christian worship; the posture, dress, mannerisms, and behavior of the worship leader can modify the meaning of the spoken or sung words in a wide variety of ways (2015, 188–189).

The way congregational music displays convictions is important communally because of the relational nature of music; each person (ostensibly) takes ownership of the activity and consequently of the perceived meaning of the music. The discursive ethics of congregational song are not configured by musical style and lyrical text alone but also by the "performative utterances" (Ingalls 2018, 50, drawing from Austin 1962) and performance practices (Steuernagel 2018) employed by the congregation and its leaders in the ritual negotiation of power dynamics in the activity of congregational singing. Indeed, the bodily interactions of the musical participants with each other as well as the music contributes significantly to the discursive power of music in worship (see Myrick 2017, for instance). Monique Ingalls has suggested that an important aspect of the efficacy of congregational singing is the use of "authenticating gestures" (such as facial expressions, bodily movements, postures, and so on) by worship leaders and music ministers (Ingalls 2011, 2018). These gestures "perform into being" an affective attitude that facilitates the full involvement of the congregation in the activity of communal music-making.

Music is encountered in myriad ways and may be understood as an activity, a text, a context, a performance, an artifact, or all of the above (see Cook 2014). Moore's distinction between language alone and musical performance allows space for distinction between words and their meanings. While Moore agrees that some words in worship are illocutionary (that is, they do what they say), he argues that musical worship is non-illocutionary, in that it is *mediated*. Indeed, his examination allows space for disagreement and miscommunication, and it lets reception matter as much as delivery in determining musical and linguistic meaning.

Nekola contends that it is largely through reception that the meaning of the mediated information is created and that receptive acts are in turn the means by which communities, cultures, and societies are made (2015, 11–14)—a concept that is helpful here. When a certain style or genre of music is performed in a discrete community that has an established pattern of meaning-making, there can be some degree of a shared world of meaning even though this meaning is unstable because of the diversity of values and convictions held by those constructing it. Yet what about the general *lack* of agreement relayed above? What of CJ's understanding of musical genre's meaning that is completely antithetical to that of the Lakeshore congregation? Perhaps even more pressing, what about marginalized communities that exist within other such communities who perceive musical meanings altogether differently?

The Dingman Hypothesis: Musical Genre and the Means of Determination

During the spring of 2014, shortly after my first child was born, one of my wife's best friends came to visit us in Los Angeles where we were living at the time. After church one Sunday, we were discussing some of what we had experienced and, as was our custom, "debriefing." Our friend, who is a lesbian Christian, noted with some sadness that she knew she would never be fully welcomed in the church we attended. This came as something of a surprise to us, as we were unaware of any position by the church on the matter of lesbian-gay-bisexual-transgender-queer (LGBTQ+) affirmation, and so we asked her how she knew. "Because of the music," she said. Seeing our puzzled looks, she continued. "I liked the music. That's the kind of music I want to worship to. But I know that churches that play that kind of music are not gay affirming."

"The Dingman Hypothesis," as we came to call it in honor of our friend, impelled my first ethnographic study of music in churches. During the winter and spring of 2015, I visited the twenty-five most popular non-denominational churches in Los Angeles as rated by YELP. I chose YELP as a way of gaining a cross section of churches, and I selected non-denominational because that was the criterion of our friend's declaration. What I found was that the Dingman Hypothesis was 95.34 percent accurate. Those churches that were "open but not affirming" of queer identities performed contemporary worship music (more specifically, the subgenre of Modern Worship as defined by Ingalls, Mall, and Nekola 2013), and those that were affirming performed older, "praise and worship" music, with only one exception. Further, during interviews for that project, I found that our friend's perception was widely shared by LGBTQ+ individuals, suggesting that agreement on how genre communicates values and convictions in churches may be achieved by groups who gather around other sources of agreement first (Myrick 2015).[11]

That communities form around shared conventions of musical meaning is undeniable, yet whether these communities are formed around musical meaning or around a different shared form of life that also informs their sense of musical meaning is less clear. As the Dingman Hypothesis suggests, LGBTQ persons did not form as a community because they agreed on what Modern Worship communicated as a genre; rather, they agreed as a community on what those styles and genres meant because of personal experiences. Indeed, it suggests that musical communities form within—or in opposition to—other communities that are themselves formed around discursive agreement on certain values and convictions, although musical meaning is an important site of discourse for those communities.

Controlling Discourse: The Shadow Side of Genre and Musical Meaning

For congregants whose acceptance in certain churches is more certain, the ways in which musical genre and style communicate values and convictions is less dire but still very important. Later in my conversation with Heather and Lacey at SXSW, the subject of musical style came up in response to my question about music's function in church. As referenced in the Introduction, their responses are telling, and they illustrate the difficulty inherent in applying generic markers to determine ethical values and convictions. A closer examination of their comments will help draw this out.

> L: So, when my parents told me as a kid, "Okay, you're a music major, you have to sing Christian music and that's how you worship God with your talents. That's how you give it back." I thought that was so fucking boring, because all that music was so boring. . . . [T]here's no emotion there. It's so completely lifeless. And so, "regular" music, you could say it saved me in that sense. It was like, I saved myself from death, constantly searching for new all the time; the way other people were searching in the Bible for

answers, I was searching for music. I'[ve] served on worship teams for years, and it wasn't until I was on worship teams that I felt like worship was fakey. We were talking about creating these emotional arcs for people, like, "we've got this fast song and we ramp them all up, and then we bring it into the really moving, orchestral pieces," and then we'd slow it down for prayer, and during altar calls there's this background music that's supposed to, like, make you feel contemplative. [It] is just manipulative. . . . I still have a lot of cynicism about that, and I still serve on like, every month or two, my church does a contemplative service and that's the only time that I really participate in that kind of thing, because it's difficult.

H: That's what I've been wrestling with too. I come from a place of ex-cynicism. I love Hillsong, and I remember going to these church services and again, they just had this set playlist, and it was just, "rise to the climactic moment, then downfall." I guess where my tension comes in is, "Ok, what's important in this? Is the intelligence important, is the emotion important?" Like, surely God did create the emotions, so surely they do have a role, so that's where my questioning is coming in where I want to have grace.

Several things stick out about Heather and Lacey's exchange that will help this account of musical genres' discursive function. First, while both women are of similar age and background, each interprets the meaning and function of the same musical genre differently: Lacey feels that contemporary worship songs are "fucking boring," "fakey," and emotionless, causing her to become deeply cynical, while Heather, sharing her cynicism, disagrees about the emotional content of contemporary worship music (specifically referencing Hillsong). Lacey's reflections give voice to many common narratives that were popularized during the "worship wars"—such as emotional manipulation by worship leaders and contemporary music ministers and her comments give evidence of the ongoing destruction of both the worship wars discourse and the ways that discourse has assigned certain meanings of value and conviction to certain genres. Against the backdrop of division that their responses had set up, I then asked them, "Does music connect people in church?"

L: Growing up in the evangelical church, I felt like it was meant to be a personal connection between me and God, and they would tell us, "Close your eyes, it's just you and God, sing to God." [I have a friend who's an atheist now] and she's said, "One thing I really miss is singing with other people."

> I go to the Episcopal church now, and it's like, we don't sing those same types of songs; we sing hymns. And for whatever reason hymns cross the intellectual divide for me, the theology is much richer . . . but it's the singing with other people.

Heather tilted her head, thinking.

> H: I have heard the argument where, contemporary worship today, in our culture, well like she said, is about you and God. And then you look at the hymns, everybody saying the same thing, it's the same type of tone, or whatever, and that makes it communal. *But for me personally, like I've been in both settings, and in settings where it has been more about the relationship between you and God, and not had the communal aspect, I've actually felt closer community [there]. . . . [I]n other scenarios where I've been, where you have the hymns, I personally don't connect with that community, . . . I don't personally connect with anyone doing that.*

The effects of the worship wars discourse are more fully illuminated by this second exchange between the two women, revealing how that discourse shaped the way many North American Protestant Christians understand musical genres in worship. Thinking carefully about Lacey's comments reveals some of the values and convictions that she considers to be mediated by contemporary worship music: emotionalism divorced from authentic expressions of faith, adherence to unoriginally replicating current fashions and trends for the sake of popularity, hyper-individualism, and so on. Heather's reflection raises important questions that trouble Lacey's interpretations: Is the emotionalism of contemporary worship music necessarily always divorced from authentic expressions of faith? Heather's comment, "Surely God did create the emotions, so surely they do have a role," suggests that dismissal of a given music on charges of emotionalism is short-sighted (as is further evidenced by Lacey's self-contradiction). Against charges of hyper-individualism, Heather contends that she feels "more connected to those around her" in contemporary worship settings, even though the worship experience is framed as being more individualistic. Their comments and the arguments implicit in them demonstrate the ideological divide that was a prominent feature of the worship wars, and this perceived dichotomy of emotion/individualism versus intellect/community was a hallmark of the discourse surrounding them.

Important for my purpose in relaying this exchange, both women believed that the *function of musical discourse and discourse about music is to build community*: Heather said, "[Music] connects me with other people"; Lacey said, "It's a shared experience . . . people's heart and emotion that you can hear and empathize with." It is here that music is most like language, as Feld and Fox suggest; they both fulfill humanity's need for connection even as they generate that need (1994, 1999; cf. Cavell 1999). It is this deep need for relationships that gives music its power both to create and destroy.

Music is not the only significant discursive means by which people negotiate relational power structures, nor is genre, as I have just described it, the only way to think about musical meaning-making. Indeed, non-musical language surrounding musical genre—the means by which genres are often determined in actuality—is as important as the sonority of the music itself, often being the means by which generic meaning is established. Drawing from Porter again, the way we *talk about* music is often as ethically significant as the music itself. As philosopher Stanley Cavell argues in his epochal tome *The Claim of Reason* (1999), human beings fulfill their basic need for community via language; societies and communities are built around shared concepts and the words that are their forms of life. He draws this out with his humorous example of the man who calls his hamsters by making the sounds and expressions commonly associated with pain (88–89). In so doing, Cavell presents us with the underlying human need for language and communication by asking rhetorically, why are we so unsettled by the idea of someone who seems to violate the conventions of communicating pain by applying these same utterances to summon hamsters? It is because we need language in order to form relationships, the core of what it is to be human (93–98). Yet language is profoundly unstable, and as the example of "hamster man" suggests, we experience great anxiety about our inability to control the meaning of words.

Tragically, such anxiety often compels us to engage in destructive discursive—and indeed, even physical—practices (see Cheng 2020). We need agreement in order to form relationships and develop communities, yet we cannot ultimately control the agency of the other people with whom we desire to have relationships. So, often if there is misunderstanding or disagreement over what language means, relationships are severed. Furthermore, distrust and anxiety may *cause* such misunderstandings and agreements, as suggested by Cavell's analysis of Othello's killing Desdemona because of his inability to control or fully know her (beyond what he knew of himself) in the final section of *The Claim of Reason*, "Between Acknowledgment and Avoidance" (1999).

Cavell suggests that our words at once reveal us and open us up to the possibility of others' self-worlds, challenging our own sufficiency in the forms of life that shared language and musical meaning entails. Our knowledge of the world is also our knowledge of ourselves, varying and constant as our language. Our words, then, confront us with ourselves—with our knowledge of what we know and what we do not know, or do not know we know, or what possible experiences we can have—and expose us to others. Ultimately then, knowledge and language are not ours alone to possess for that will eliminate our self from our world (1999, 351). Instead, our competency in the shared forms of life that language demands/facilitates/exposes is configured in the relationships that human beings have with one another.

This realization of the relational need for humans and relational nature of language clarifies what impelled the worship wars and what made them so destructive; musical discourse and discourse about musical meaning *built communities that were, by their very nature, mutually exclusive, because they were interwoven with people's deepest values and convictions, on one hand, and the subsequent fears and anxiety over issues of control and agreement about meaning, on the other.* When values and convictions were ascribed to certain genres, relationships were formed or severed. More than that, the term "worship wars" and its attendant martial metaphors (barrage, assault, winner/loser, camp, marched, and so on) contributed to this destructive milieu.[12] However individual these convictions may be, they are formed in the context of community and are inextricably concerned with the flourishing of that community—sometimes in opposition to others. Just as music is at its core an ordered relationship between pitches, timbres, units of time, and so on, so the ethics of style and the convictions that inform it are inherently relational.

As Jeff R. Warren points out in *Music and Ethical Responsibility* (2014), the relational component of music itself, coupled with the necessarily relational activity of music-making, establishes the context wherein music and musical style carries ethical import for its participants (1–11). Such responsibility transcends the marketplace notion of paying for disposable musical artifacts and reaches into the world examined by Rommen; musical style has a discursive ethical element that is activated and empowered simultaneously by the relational power of music and the subsequent engagement with it by individuals who are communally and relationally responsible to each other. But when this responsibility is placed into conflict with responsibility to other convictions and commitments, especially theological and ethical claims, as is common in Christian communities, unethical relationships result. Indeed, the suggestion that congregations were at war with each other (or within themselves) provided a violent impulse toward those who identified with a different set of sonic and social values and convictions. Thinking with Cavell reveals that these verbal acts of world-making often have tragic, destructive consequences. As I hope is clear by now, the collateral damage of the verbal and musical combat is still present, and the fallout is very real.[13]

Yet there is more to this discussion than can be accounted for by an appeal to meaningful agreement-cum-community. Linguistic and interpersonal conflicts regarding genre and style for Christian communities are driven by the need to authentically express personal values and convictions. Clearly, musical meaning is configured by the way participants respond to the musical activity they are engaged in. As such, meaning itself is established on pre-determined commitments, and as I show in Chapter 2, those commitments are intensely affective and relational.

2
Formation
Affection, Emotion, and the Problem of Authenticity

I sat in the breezeway at Common Grounds coffee shop in Waco on a cold January morning. Seating in the small, "rural hipster"–inspired establishment was sparse, so Kim and I decided to sit in the semi-enclosed breezeway adjacent to the main seating area to avoid the clamor of the many patrons inside. An undergraduate social work major, Kim was a volunteer intern at Harris Creek who often led worship at one of the two campuses. In response to my initial question, "What does music do?" *Kim answered similarly to many others:* "It connects people from different walks of life and brings them together with some shared experience." *She paused, then continued,* "Or, it connects emotions that you can't put words to, so internally and externally." *When I asked her what she meant by that, she clarified:*

> [In] my experiences, I tend to only focus on positive emotions, and music forces me to feel and acknowledge the feelings that are beyond just those superficial ones that are a lot easier to feel. So, I think part of it's being able to write about joy and heartache and pain and goals. Things that people universally feel. And so it brings people together through those emotions.

When I asked her how this understanding of music influences her experiences of others through music, she explained,

> I think I see people on a more vulnerable level. But they see me more vulnerably if I'm the one singing, or something like that. Then also, they're sharing their experience and their emotions. So, there's a level of danger to it. Like, you have the potential, if you're putting yourself out there, to be hurt or anything like that. I think I see people just a little bit more honestly, which I appreciate.

Sensing my interest, or perhaps just wanting to clarify, she continued.

Music for Others. Nathan Myrick, Oxford University Press (2021). © Oxford University Press.
DOI: 10.1093/oso/9780197550625.003.0003

> I mean I think we walk around wearing masks all the time. Like, a lot of times we just [think we know what people want to see] "so, I'm gonna be this." You know technology and social media; all those things don't exactly help. [Laughs] So, music kind of pulls the mask back a little bit. And you can usually tell [if someone's not being honest in their music]. If a person's really being honest with their music and themselves, you get to see a little bit of who they actually are. Seeing beyond the facade.

Affect, Reason, and "Emotional Intelligence"

Music and emotion are often linked in everyday life. In addition to discursive communication, as I have been arguing, music connects us to others by interacting with our emotions. Kathleen Marie Higgins has noted that there have been three historical models for understanding how music interacts with human emotions: as imitating (or "mirroring"), invoking ("arousing"), or expressing (2011, 63–79). Her observations are supported by my research, although her suggestion—"saying that music makes one self-aware is uncommon" (119)—is challenged by it.

In response to my question, "What does music do," Bev from Lakeshore said "[It] starts to tap into the emotional side [of human life]." When I asked Mary, a Fuller student interviewed at SXSW, if music influenced her sense of well-being, she noted that music can uniquely *express* emotions: "Sometimes that's the only medium where people authentically express emotions," and because of that unique expressive ability we are able to feel alongside others; "it gives me a snapshot into . . . the emotions that [the singer or writer or performer is] feeling."

Others noted that music was able to invoke emotions, both positively and negatively: Lakeshore's Senior Pastor, Kyndall Rothaus, responding to the question of well-being, said, "Music . . . unlocks emotions in me that I didn't even know [were] possible. . . . There are certain songs that make you cry . . . [but] in terms of emotional well-being, I think that music can reach a place that words can't reach yet." Still others, such as Aaron, a hospice chaplain in his early thirties who attended Lakeshore, said that music both expresses and invokes emotion: "It's a way that we're able to express ourselves, to emote in a lot of ways. It can also be a source of comfort. So, it is a way that we emote but it's also a way that we kind of can bring emotions into our lives. We can be affected by music as well, which can change our disposition in one way or the other."

It is overwhelmingly clear that music is *valued* by many for its ability to engage human emotions on a level that words cannot. This valuation of emotion implies that music's value is often determined by its emotional abilities: as Lacey put it, music is bad when it is emotionless, when "there's no emotion"; but as Dan, a Harris Creek youth director said, it is good when "it expresses authentic emotions."

An essential part of music's way of being in the world, then, is its affective power: as expression, as invocation, and as space for emotional interaction with others. This suggests that emotion and affection are (1) formed and developed through action and participation in musical activities, and (2) employed in the process of configuring relational postures and attitudes toward self and others; therefore they influence human volition and agency. In a word, music is formational, as the following pages demonstrate.

Music's formational power is affective and emotional as well as intellectual, and it is relational as well as individual. This is to say that while these elements are often separable for the sake of analysis, they are not separated in real life; a heart, lungs, and liver are analytically understood to be different, yet none can perform its function alone. Extending the metaphor further, it is quite obvious that if one or all three were removed from a body, that body would die. In the same way, while bad analysis fails to recognize difference, bad theorizing fails to recognize how concepts, elements, or experiences relate. Musical worship forms intellectually, but doctrinal pedagogy and intellectual formation alone do not account for all of the ways that people are formed in musical worship.

Narrative Formation Ethics: Story, Ritual, and Character

Ethical reflection and study from the disciplines of liturgical and practical theology have largely sought to evaluate the character formation that occurs in Christian worship from the perspective of neo-Aristotelian ethics, primarily by taking the formative power of *narrative* as central to this task. The following pages affirm this foundation yet trouble it in ways suggesting that a nuanced understanding of Christian formation requires much more than solely an engagement (no matter how prolonged) with narrative.

Ethics-as-character-formation through worship draws heavily on the theories of virtue ethics that can trace their origin to the ancient Greek philosophers Damon, Plato, and Aristotle, through the patristic Augustine, medieval Aquinas, and the philosophy cum doctrine of *ethos* as reinterpreted by the modern philosopher Alasdair McIntyre (Ursu 2009; Hauerwas 1974, 1975, cf. 2015; Seasolitz 2012). This understanding of ethics as character places the emphasis of ethical scholarship and praxis on the practices that build character, not the crises that define it (Hauerwas and Wells 2011, for example). The worship service plays a foundational role in this development of character in that it is a regular ritual that has defined and explicit moral values built into it by both association and representation. In a mutually constitutive way, liturgical scholars argue that worship is ethical in that it forms ethical character and fulfills ethical responsibilities (Arndt 1960; Sayers 1961; Saliers 1998 [1979]; Rossi 1979; Hauerwas and Wells, 2011; Seasolitz 2012). Additionally, character formation through worship establishes the worshipper's perspectives and relationships: to other worshippers, to the world, and to the divine (from a Christian perspective, Suggate 2002, 56; Müller 2006, 645; from a Jewish perspective, Kadushin 1964, 5–6, for example).

Scholars differ, however, as to how they understand this ethics-as-character formation to occur. On the one hand, Christian character is formed by listening to the stories that inform the faith and orient the self toward living these stories (Rossi 1979; Saliers 1979; Müller 2006; Hauerwas and Wells 2011, for example). On the other hand, ethical character is formed through participation in the ritual and activity of worship in the celebration of the sacraments (Wannenwetsch 2004 [1997]; Suggate 2002, for example). Hauerwas and Wells connect both as activities of formation, as action and as listening (2011).

Two things must be said regarding liturgical character formation theory. First, a crucial component to the flourishing of the individual in virtue theory (which liturgical character formation theories draw heavily from) is the flourishing of the community. According to MacIntyre, "My good as a man is one and the same as those of others with whom I am bound up in community" (1978, 193). Second, such a community's flourishing depends on the formation of virtuous character in the lives of the individuals rather than on the ability to determine what the moral duty demanded by natural law must be (193).

These two salient features of virtue ethics begin to suggest how ethical formation of both individuals and communities can be understood to take place through the activity of musical worship. If musical discourses and activities construct affective and relational communities even as they proclaim values and convictions, then it stands to reason that such formation contributes significantly to the study of ethics from the perspective of character formation. As James F. Caccamo has argued, "Ritual singing itself is a set of particular and regular religiously responsive performances that shape the ways in which individuals respond to God and neighbor outside of the ritual event" (2004, ix), and thus they have ethical implications. Caccamo, in his study of contemporary Roman Catholic ritual song's ethical import, describes virtue ethics like this,

> Virtue ethics focus[es] on the creation of persons and communities who are able to act dependably in ways that instantiate truth and happiness. Acts are not unimportant in the virtue approach, of course. But the importance of any single action is understood to be subordinate to the extent to which that action both creates and is the result of a person who is attempting to enact ultimate commitments in daily life. The virtue model of the Christian moral life focuses on the creation of people who incarnate Gospel. (177)

Drawing on the work of Saliers, Hauerwas, Rossi, and others, Caccamo's work argues for the place of ritual song in the formation of individual moral character and identity, offering much in helpfully moving this discussion forward. He, too, connects the affections engendered by music to character formation and argues that this is ethically significant. By using virtue ethics, he is able to affirm and support the liturgical practices of Roman Catholic churches while simultaneously offering a means of locating music as an equal player in that activity, although he understands music's role to be one of support. Additionally, in his treatment of virtue ethics, he rightly notes that "moral life," as a category applied to the study of character formation arising from liturgical practice, is often far too concerned with personal and "individual action and identity" (22). Instead, he argues that ethical formation (he calls it "virtue") is inextricably social and communal. Finally, he argues that the formation that occurs through practice and participation in ritual Christian worship calls Christians to respond in gospel-informed ways, thereby placing the emphasis on responsiveness (218 ff).

Narrative virtue ethics opens up our understanding of how individual affections and the affective and relational communities formed in musical worship are ethically significant by focusing our attention on how the development of character is vital for ethical action. Furthermore, the emphasis of communal flourishing and well-being is an important turn away from individuated conceptions of flourishing, although as Caccamo rightly notes the impulse for individual focus remains for many scholars of virtue.

Yet musical activity is more than simply sound, and musical worship is more than diatonic discourse. As helpful as it is, Christian narrative character formation ethics goes only part way in providing the foundation for theorizing about musical ethics; several critiques of liturgical formation ethics are in need of explication.

First, liturgical formation ethics come perilously close to confusing formation with conformity, such that the real differences between communities and individuals is offered only lip service. Second, and proceeding from the first, liturgical character formation ethics through worship are often overly deterministic, assuming that if the Christian story is rightly engaged, virtuous character will be formed in the lives of the faithful. This presents a number of epistemological problems, with perhaps the most significant being who determines what Christian character is. Certainly, many have laid claim to this knowledge or one of its analogs, as evidenced by the sheer proliferation of denominations and sects of Protestantism (to say nothing of the myriad localized Christian communities the world over), each basing Christian character on its own understanding of "orthodoxy."[1] This observation presents another problem that can be framed as the question of how orthodoxy is related to character. For example, Constance Cherry notes the importance of orthodoxy for forming Christian character and impulses for Christian action in her practical book, *The Music Architect*: "Right worship (*orthodoxy* . . .) leads to right action (*orthopraxy*) which, in turn, leads to right affection (*orthocardia*)" (2016, 33).[2] While on the face of it this statement is fairly innocuous, significant problems arise when we realize that each denomination or even community has a particular claim to orthodoxy that is often constructed in opposition to another such claim, so appealing to ecclesial authority on matters of doctrine does not give a satisfactory account of the goodness of each doctrine that lays claim to "orthodoxy."

Indeed, one of the central problems with claims to orthodoxy is that many authors and leaders often use such claims to invoke a universal orthodoxy that precludes all others by definition—thus leading to the conflicts I described in Chapter 1. Indeed, unless an ethical theory is able to interrogate ecclesial authority and claims to orthodoxy it will be unable to offer any means of evaluating the ethical significance of music in Christian communities beyond its unqualified affirmation. Bernd Wannenwetsch's *Political Worship* (2004) is emblematic of this dilemma, and his contention that worship can be neither ethical nor unethical offers no way of critiquing unjust worship; instead, it concludes that worship will inevitably make Christians exemplary citizens (359). This conclusion seems to work against an ethic of anything beyond affirming the status quo—despite his assertions to the contrary.[3] What of societies whose polity is at odds with "the good" as revealed in Christian worship? While Wannenwetsch's confidence that history will see as exemplary the worshipper whose actions oppose the prevailing social climate, such future historical certainty offers little by way of compulsion for good activity in the face of popular injustice—to say nothing of the need for internal critique of ecclesial politics.

Returning to my bodily system metaphor from earlier, in the same way that a human body will die if a heart, a liver, or the lungs are given primacy over the others, orthodoxy cannot be determined without a thorough account of orthopraxy and orthocardia; the Body will die if its members are broken down to their constitutive parts in isolation. Orthodoxy cannot be the sole interrogator of praxis and affection; each must read the other in a mutually constitutive, triadic manner.

Third, liturgical character formation ethics seems to take a diminished view of human agency in moral action, on the one hand, while disproportionately elevating that agency, on the other. On the first hand, while I affirm without reservation the need for formation before moments of crisis, moral action still requires human volition in that moment of crisis—to say nothing of the ability to recognize when such a moment approaches. Indeed, if well founded, our responses may be more ethical than otherwise, but such an assertion does not offer a means of evaluating context, specifics, and other mitigating factors aside from the assurance that Christians will know what is good because of their formation as Christians. On the second hand, as James M. Gustafson points out, each individual's agency is constrained by the agency of others: by society, by relationships, by power, by access to means, and so on (1981, 174). My ability to act ethically, no matter how well formed my character may be, is limited by my existence in a discrete place and time and by the discrete relationships I need to flourish.

Finally, narrative formation ethics falls victim to the same pitfalls that discourse ethics encounters when music is considered due to its strong reliance on language as the primary means of forming character. In the same way that the instability of language and therefore discursive meaning unsettles our assurance of imaginatively inhabiting shared musical life-worlds, so reliance on shared understandings of the Christian narrative to form character in accordance with "orthodoxy" suffers the same fate. This is especially pronounced when music's affective way of being in the world is considered, as music affects the meaning of the very words that orthodoxy relies on for stability. The mere act of musical participation in Christian worship where the songs contain orthodox lyrics tells us nothing about the goodness nor justice of the communities that form around these musical acts.

However, I hope that it is evident that I am not proposing to throw out character formation altogether, as its merits are plainly evident. Rather, I am proposing that it does not go far enough and that more needs to be said about *how we can evaluate* the formation that takes place through musical activity. Consequently, this means of evaluation should also afford a means of evaluating the goodness, that is, the ethicalness, of musical activity in Christian communities—and by extension the goodness of "orthodoxy."

Musical Worship and Formation

As a church that has a long and complex history and a series of tangled affiliations, Harris Creek Baptist Church proved a fascinating lens through which to examine music's affective formation. Harris Creek is one of the older Baptist congregations in the Waco area, having been founded in 1880. The church is affiliated most closely with the Baptist General Convention of Texas (BGCT) but is also affiliated to a lesser extent with the Cooperative Baptist Fellowship (CBF) and the Southern Baptist Convention (SBC). Drew Greenway, Worship and Care Pastor at Harris Creek, says that they are "Bad Baptists"; they send money only for missions to these organizations and do not participate in the conventions or assemblies.

I met Drew for coffee at Pinewood Coffee Roasters in early December 2017. We had spoken on several occasions before and had developed good rapport with each other. My conversations with Drew, in addition to discussing my primary research questions, touched on his philosophy of music in worship as well as some of the background of the church. Having served at Harris

Creek for ten years,[4] Drew was the longest tenured staff person at the church and was thus able to speak with some authority to both the history and philosophy of worship in the church. In response to my question, "What role do you see music playing in Harris Creek's worship services?" Drew's first response was "That's a big question!" After gathering his thoughts, Drew responded that he saw music's role at Harris Creek as having emotional impact that combined with the meaning of the lyrics

> to give people truth to sing throughout their entire lifetime. I use this example all the time; my grandmother had Alzheimer's and died. She forgot—she read her Bible like crazy and she loved music like crazy, and by the end of her life she couldn't remember any Bible verses, she couldn't remember anybody's name, but she would remember lines and lines and lines of hymns and songs. That really helped me define something I already knew, which was, it's our job—liturgy's job is to give people a voice for the different seasons of their life. . . . And that's why we're kind of halfway into the church calendar. I think giving people some rhythm to their lives, some meaning to these services that are kind of added to the normal Sunday routine. [For example] Advent; you know, we never did Advent growing up. I just knew we sang Christmas songs when it was around Christmas time. It wasn't ever this, like, "Holy expectation [of] Christ coming," and what he's going to do in the world. That's some cool stuff to give people [to think about].

Drew framed his comments about music's role in church by emphasizing the didactic nature of musical worship's meaningfulness as being more important than its affective power. While not explicitly addressing formation, his comments suggest at least two significant themes that are both well established and also important for my purposes here. First, Drew's philosophy that liturgy should give people a meaningful, narrative guide throughout their lives agrees with much of the literature on formation in worship—that it is by engaging the Christian narrative and living intentionally into it that the faithful are formed (see Saliers 1998 [1979]; Hauerwas 1975, 2015; Hauerwas and Wells 2011, for example). By embracing the liturgical calendar for its worship planning, Harris Creek (along with many other churches) has sought to provide a broad, far-reaching structure by which its congregants can make feelingful connections between the seasons of their lives and the story and theology of the Christian faith.

Music participates in this formational activity in a number of ways. Martha Nussbaum's work offers a fruitful means of weaving together the threads of formation with emotion and affection through music.[5] In her 2001 book *Upheavals of Thought*, she uses psychoanalytical theory to understand how emotions affect human reasoning, arguing that emotions involve important judgements about persons, events, and ideas (19). She further suggests that emotion is meaningless unless it is narratalogically constructed, meaning that human feelings are always connected to stories and experiences and the ways we make sense of our lives through them (236). Importantly, she specifically relates narrative emotions and judgment making to music, arguing that music enlivens our deep emotions that influence our thinking and judgments (259–265).

Considered in the context of musical worship, Harris Creek's embrace of the liturgical calendar merges narrative meaning with emotion (although Drew was careful to note the meaning of the songs over and above their feeling). James K. A. Smith's (2009) connection of affections to character formation and reasoning helps to unpack Drew's reflection on his grandmother's ability to recite lines and lines of hymns even after she had lost her ability to remember the Bible passages she memorized so zealously or the names of family members. In *Desiring the Kingdom*, Smith argues that people are most profoundly shaped by the activities that they love (46 ff). He further suggests that human beings are formed more profoundly by what they love than by what they think—that is to say, *character is formed by our affections more than by our reasoning* (47–50). Instead, our reasoning is *informed* by our affections, and we justify that which we love (51–55). Yet Drew's comments also beg important questions that point to one of the central arguments of this chapter: that *music* forms and shapes affections in ways that afford meaning-making and communal and identity formation—even when those ways are unrecognized or unacknowledged.

How is it that Drew's grandmother remembered the lines and tunes of hymns but not names of family nor passages of scripture? Indeed, it would be dubious to conclude that Drew's grandmother loved hymns more than her family. Yes, our affections and desires shape us, and as humans, our reasoning is often in support of what we love (Smith 2009, 51; Caccamo 2004); yet, as Daniel Levitin (2007), Oliver Sacks (2007), and others contend, we remember our loves more clearly when they are accompanied by music. Drew's grandmother had been formed through her habitual love of hymns in such a way that even after many faculties of memory had been ravaged by

Alzheimer's she could still recall and be comforted by the hymns she loved because their lyrics were set to music. Thinking with the scholars mentioned in this paragraph and especially the reflections of my conversation partners, it is music's ability to engender affections and enliven emotion that facilitates this deep formation.

However, the ravages of diseases such as Alzheimer's or other forms of dementia cannot be the sole describers of music's formative properties, because it is precisely the *loss* of relational memory that makes such diseases so tragic. While we may take some comfort in the fact that loved ones who cannot remember who we are or why they know us can seemingly be re-enlivened by a favorite piece of music (and I have been so comforted in dealing with dementia in my family), that comfort is increased exponentially when our loved ones briefly recognize us in those moments of musical memory (as noted by the scholars mentioned above). What is significant about this observation is that it directs our attention toward the *reason* we appreciate this aspect of music's way of being in the world: that it has the ability—no matter how briefly and limited—to restore our relationships with those we love whose relational abilities have left them prematurely, when we see them enjoying something we knew they enjoyed before their illness, when we share those moments of mutual recognition.

Emotional Intelligence and the Relational Self

An important and often under-examined aspect of this formational property of musical activity is that of relational identity construction through emotional experiences. Heather's comments from Chapter 1—that "[music makes me more] emotionally intelligent. It makes me more emotionally aware of myself"—sheds light on this perspective of the importance of music in identity formation. Nussbaum's work is again helpful in unpacking the idea of "emotional intelligence." Simply stated, "emotional intelligence" describes the ability to identify one's own emotions and to empathetically identify the emotions of another (Salovey and Meyer 1990, 185), and it makes an explicit claim to the connection of emotion to reason and, drawing from Nussbaum, judgments.[6] Other scholars, such as John Pellitteri et al. (1999) have connected emotional intelligence to music. In their article, "Music: The Sounds of Emotional Intelligence," Pellitteri et al. argued that music-making and listening can teach emotional intelligence to children and middle schoolers (their immediate subject matter), helping them recognize their own emotions and the emotions of others. Another study by Resnicow et al. (2004) concluded from analyzing a focus group that identification of emotion in music corresponded significantly to emotional intelligence (145), although they did not conclude that the correspondence was causal.

Whether or not music has a causal relationship to emotional intelligence (if such a thing even exists; see Barrett 2017), people engage music as if it did. Crucially, the second part of Heather's comment—"but it also connects me with other people"—indicates that such awareness and identity construction is interwoven with an awareness of others. Heather is not alone in this assessment. Again and again, my conversation partners described seeing and identifying with the emotional states of others—as well as their own—as being a hallmark of music in general and music for Christian worship in particular: hearing the emotions of others, identifying with them, feeling alongside others, and so on. The significance of these reflections is helpfully drawn out by thinking with Charles Taylor's idea of "social imaginaries," the "ways in which [people] imagine their social existence, how they fit together with others, how things go between them and their fellows" (2007, 171). Read through the lens of Taylor's formulation, the idea of "emotional intelligence" reveals how people imagine music to form and inform their ability to relate to others in emotional and consequently affective ways. Thinking further, the ability to imagine (rather than to theorize, per Taylor) the social relationships we embody through musical listening and participation allows us to (imaginatively) encounter others in emotionally profound ways.

Emotional Well-Being: On the Importance of Musical Ritual

Fieldwork at Harris Creek, November 5, 2017, McGregor, Texas. *The band finishes "Brave" and the worship leader transitions into the next song with "Amen. Let's continue singing this morning." The band moves seamlessly into "O Praise the Name (Anastasis)" by Hillsong Worship (2015), also in the key of E-flat. Following "O Praise the Name," the leader reminds the congregation that this Sunday is All Saints Day, a day when Christians remember those who have "gone before" them, inspiring or instructing them either through personal contact or through sharing heroic stories of the saints. The practice of remembering All Saints Day is not common in the Baptist tradition that Harris Creek belongs to, and she makes a point to clearly and simply explain the significance of the day. She then invites the congregation to make their way to the front of the sanctuary and place one of the poppy flowers lying on a table in front of the stage into one of the vases on the table during the next song in remembrance of a deceased friend or family member. The keyboardist affects a pad (textured drone) in G underneath this explanation, and holds the pad while the congregation is led through a responsive reading of Hebrews 12:1. At the close of the reading, the band strikes up "Faithful to the End," by Paul and Hannah McClure (2016), joining the pad to play the song. As they do so, two lines begin to form in each of the aisles leading to the stage, as congregants place poppies in the vases in memory of their lost loved ones. This ceremony continues throughout the song, and I notice that several worshippers are crying as they place their poppies in the vase.*

Perhaps sensing the meaningfulness of the moment or perhaps scheduled in anticipation of its effect, the band transitions without pause into the final song of the set, "Before the Throne of God Above," a public domain hymn texted by Charitie Lees Bancroft in 1863 and re-popularized by Keith and Kristen Getty, as well as other worship leaders in the early twenty-first century. The congregation continues placing poppies as they sing heartily along to "Before the Throne." The band vamps on the refrain as the last of the congregation completes the ceremony, and the worship leader invites us to be seated.

The connection between emotion and affective formation was on display in several instances during my fieldwork, such as the worship service from All Saints Sunday at Harris Creek. Examining that event—especially the ritual of the poppies—provides valuable insight into how meaning and emotion converge in human bodies during musical activity that forms social and relational imaginaries.

There are several aspects of the ritual of the poppies that make it an affective and formative experience. First, the congregation was encouraged to acknowledge and indeed embrace their emotions, especially in relation to others; to process and grieve the loss of family and friends during the ritual of placing poppies in the vases while singing as a congregation. Second, this encouragement of emotional expression was extended by coupling music with this act of grieving. As Dan, the youth director I met during my visit on All Saints Sunday, explained in a later conversation, music coupled with that particular ritual was designed to minister to the emotional health of the congregation and to form (or re-form, as the case may be) healthy emotional postures. In response to my question, "Can music heal?" Dan responded,

> Yes, totally, totally. I can even think of an example of seeing people in church that I know are going through really hard times. Recently there was a nineteen-year-old in our church that passed away in his sleep. I saw his mom in church next week and as I see her worshipping I can feel that, [I] can see that maybe [she's] singing the things she wants to say or wants to think. And not like ignoring the pain. But like trusting God with the pain. So. Yes, I definitely think music can heal.

Earlier in our conversation (in response to my question "What does music do?"), Dan had spoken of music's ability to influence his emotional well-being, and in relaying this story, he connected that understanding of music's affective power to the ways that music assists in emotional healing and faith formation during worship, noting that music helps "internalize the feelings . . . [of the meaning and ideas] of the lyrics." I am not sure if Dan was explicitly referencing the ritual of the poppies in his example of the grieving mother, but it is evident that Harris Creek's ministerial staff understood music's role in the worship service as one of emotional faith formation.

However, while Drew and to a lesser extent Dan emphasized music's affective aspects in concert with the didactic content of the lyrics, that emphasis was not always shared by the congregation (although none denied the importance of the lyrics). In an email exchange I had with Carin, a woman in her mid-sixties who had attended Harris Creek for many years, she noted that while the ritual of the poppies is important for her each year, as she takes the opportunity to remember her mother's family, she did not remember what song was being sung during the ritual I had observed, although she had indeed taken part in it. In Carin's case, the affect of the music during the ritual was more important than the lyrical content of the song, indicating that an emphasis on content over affect in formation theory may be unfounded or at least overemphasized. Others shared her sentiment that the content of the lyrics (or even which song was sung) was less important during the ritual of the poppies: Kim, who had been playing acoustic guitar and singing on All Saints Sunday, noted that the ritual was beautiful and invoked a strong emotional response in her, but she did not mention the content of the song—lyrical or otherwise—in her reflection. Similarly, Tom (whose ideas are discussed in the next paragraph) said he had no idea what the song was during the ritual of the poppies, and although he himself did not lay down a poppy this year, he noted that he was glad that Harris Creek performed that ritual.

This aspect of the explicit formation that occurs in musical worship through the convergence of meaning and emotion in ritual practice is well framed by my conversation with Tom, who was interviewed at Drew's behest as part of the Harris Creek ethnography. Tom is a professor of the sociology of religion and had a well-formed and thought-out perspective on the subject of communal formation. His response to my first question, "What does music do?" echoed those of others:

> T: I think it connects to the heart in a way that is not linguistic. I think it expresses some of humanity's most compelling emotions.
>
> Author: How does it express those emotions?
>
> T: I don't know. It's one of those things where it's non-linguistic! [Laughs] So, for me music is a heart (gestures to his chest), like physically, I mean it pounds in your chest, vibrates in your chest. In a way that you don't think about verbally. You can FEEL and experience. And it can change emotions.

Tom's comment that music can change emotions is superficially obvious, but closer reflection reveals that such emotional change has both formational and moral importance. When I asked him about his experience of others in music, he responded:

> T: I think music has the ability to unite a crowd in one solid emotion. It can get us all on the same page. Get us to stop thinking about our individual selves [but to think about] our collected selves. I'm getting into sociology. So, it definitely connects people. It's a connecter. I would call it social solidarity. That's the word I would use.

I asked Tom if he thought that this kind of social solidarity had a formative aspect to it, and he said, "Absolutely." He explained his understanding in theoretical terms. Drawing from Emile Durkheim, Randall Collins, and others, he noted that ritual activity such as attending a musical concert forms social solidarity, but in the context of a Brad Paisley concert (which was the example he used in our conversation), the formation that occurs is more ephemeral than long lasting.[7] When I asked Tom about music's role in this ritual social formation, he answered in affective terms:

> T: It turns our heart. Let me think explicitly in the context of worship. So, at church this morning [we sang] "All the poor and powerless" (All Sons &

> Daughters, 2012) after a sermon on "You must look out for the marginalized." This idea of looking out for the powerless. And it [the song] turned my heart towards them . . . music can guide our feelings and emotions.

Durkheim, Collins, and others are fruitful conversation partners in understanding how rituals form social groups and individual and relational identities. However, one important consideration here propels my inquiry beyond their work: I am seeking to describe the role that *music plays* in those kinds of formation. David Hesmondhalgh's (2013) work is helpful here. Drawing on Martha Nussbaum's assertion that affection must be considered in providing an account of human flourishing (2001), Hesmondhalgh argues that public enjoyment of music provides the basis for private and public formation. Thinking alongside the assertion of Nussbaum (and others, such as Higgins) that relationships are ontological for human beings and therefore that healthy relationships are crucial for human flourishing, he suggests that it is due to this need for good relationships that music's affective power forms relational identities through habitual music making and listening (14–21, cf. 109 ff). His argument is a compounding one: we enjoy music and how it makes us feel, so we enjoy it with others, which in turn makes us enjoy it even more, and we enjoy others because of our enjoyment with music. Our mutual enjoyment spreads and becomes a public mode of affection, such as popular music concerts or dances (his examples; see also Frith 1996).

Offering further perspective on the way that music "turns our heart," as Tom called it, Jeremy S. Begbie has suggested that music may interact with human emotions and affections through what he terms "contour theory," where the sounds of the music mimic the bodily gestures associated with certain feelings, such as "cheerful" music being loud and in the upper registers, whereas "sad" music is slow, soft, and in the lower registers (2011, 342). Drawing from the work of Stephen Davies (1994), Peter Kivy (2002, 2007), and Leonard Meyer (1956), along with others, Begbie considers how music engenders "faithful feelings" in the context of musical worship. As such, building on the "classic triad," he argues that emotions are not only private affairs but are also intensely social experiences in that people recognize and relate to the emotional states of others, thus "turning our hearts towards them [others]" (in Tom's words) when the emotional experience is "faithful," that is, when it coheres with lived reality.

In addition to being profoundly affective and relational, these experiences of musical activity, both in rituals and in everyday life, are also inescapably embodied. We do not experience music or even emotion in isolation from the bodies that compose our beings. Considering this reality at length will take steps toward offering an account of music's formative properties.

Emotional Efficacy and Embodied Relationships

The ways that musical activity configures our social imaginaries affectively are complex and multi-valent. In addition to contour theory, as laid out by Begbie, Hesmondhalgh, and others, the phenomenon of entrainment is another way of getting at how music engenders emotions in human beings and connects us to others in profound ways—with the added benefit of accounting for the physical existence of music as sound that interacts with human bodies. Entrainment is the phenomenon of two independent rhythmic oscillators synchronizing their rate of oscillations when in proximity to one another without direct physical contact, provided a suitable coupling factor is present. Entrainment occurs in human beings in myriad ways, and importantly, it can occur when people listen to or make music (Clayton et al. 2005; Clayton 2013). In several laboratory experiments, musical entrainment has been found to activate the areas of the human brain thought to be associated with emotions, such that when our brain rhythms synchronize with music we experience emotional sensations (Juslin and Sloboda 2011; Trost et al. 2014; Labbe and Grandjean 2014; Aksentijevic et al. 2014; Vuilleumier and Trost 2015, for instance).

I have argued elsewhere that musical entrainment is important for understanding the emotional efficacy of musical worship (Myrick 2017). My study of worshippers at the National Worship Leader Conference in Dallas, Texas, showed that successive experiences of entrainment during musical worship heightened the emotional intensity of relational bonds in those communities, but whether those relationships were healthy depended on the negotiation of relational power during and surrounding the musical events. The theory I offered, compound ritual entrainment (CRE), suggests that through interaction with the physical phenomena of entrainment (independent rhythmic oscillatory process adjusting rate and speed [tempo] to match another's) in congregational settings of musical participation, human affections, relationships, and identity are formed and informed through regular, ritual participation in the activity of congregational song. In this theory of entrainment and formation, the independent rhythmic oscillations of human beings (biorhythms such as breathing, heartbeat, and neural processes) become "entrained," or matched up, with those of others in the context of musical participation. In this way, the music acts as the "coupling factor" for the entraining phenomenon; it does not "synchronize" with people, but rather people entrain with other people through the presence of musical rhythms.[8] The quality of this formation is contingent on the enculturation of the individual (the cultural proficiency one possesses) and the negotiation of relational power dynamics inherent in any ritual activity. Whether the experience is remembered as positive or negative is determined in part by the ritual negotiation of power dynamics in worship: between the people and God; between the worship leader and the congregation; between the congregation members themselves; between the pastor and worship leader; between the pastor and the congregation.[9]

The way that musical activity embodies our social imaginaries through entrainment also has an aesthetic characteristic to it that clarifies the points of relational contact between emotion and individual/communal formation. Jonathan Dueck, in his 2017 monograph *Congregational Music, Conflict, and Community*, argues that musical aesthetics (as distinct from style or theology) "articulate with an individual's memories of the feelingful social relationships formed around their own history of musical performance and listening" (11). He grounds his understanding of aesthetics in the real world of human musical interactions, examining the "meanings church music accrues through use over time, through individual and social memory" (14). Dueck's work emphasizes that the primary value of musical worship for his interlocutors was neither the style nor the theology but rather the *social relationships* that are formed, strengthened, and remembered through musical worship (2, 45ff.). These relationships are profoundly embodied, with the physical acts of singing and playing inhabiting an integral role in musical worship's significance—what he calls affect: "embodied feelings" (117). This embodied relationship draws out how social imaginaries are embodied in musical worship and how that embodiment is fundamental to the efficacy of both personal and relational formation.

Taking the writings of Begbie, Dueck, Hesmondhalgh, Nussbaum, Smith, Taylor and my own previous work together with the evidence presented in this chapter suggest that music interacts with embodied[10] human emotions in at least one of Higgins's three ways: music is involved in (1) expressing emotion; (2) mimicking emotion; (3) eliciting or invoking emotion—often all at the same time. Furthermore, the emotions associated with music overwhelmingly involve other people—in memory, in immediate physical contact, and in a host of other ways; this is a part of music's way of being in the world. Taking these "social imaginaries" together with Nussbaum's argument that human beings are not exclusively sentient or emotive but are both at the same time suggests that the affective aspects of music are ethically significant; reason and emotion converge in human bodies in musical activity.

These observations further clarify the ethical significance of music's role in producing affect by highlighting that the way we imagine ourselves to be in relationships with others is oriented by how we feel about them, which is informed by rationality and affections. Thinking with Smith reveals that we are formed as individuals and communities according to what we love and desire: our affections. Applying this suggestion directly to the context of musical worship reveals that music may indeed form ethical emotions in congregants and that the "feelingfulness" of musical worship is always and again an embodied and relationally formative affair.

The Problem of Authenticity and Music's Way of Being at Church

Up to this point, I have argued that an understanding of music's way of being in the world is crucial for any theorization about music's ethical significance. Drawing on both my ethnographic research and the work of other scholars, I have argued that an essential aspect of music's way of being in the world is its ability to connect people and build communities—although this formation into community is often conceived as being in opposition to another such community. I have further argued that these processes of connecting and uniting work in two ways: first, in Chapter 1, I argued that Christian communities form around shared understanding of musical meaning. I arrived at this conclusion by studying how people understood church music as a means of communicating values and convictions. Further, I argued that for many, musical meaning is configured largely by musical genre, but that these generic understandings of musical meaning were unstable, because they were subject to constant negotiation through discourse. This instability precludes ethical theorization on the premise of discourse alone yet indicates that the discourse that takes place both around and through musical activity is ethically important. Indeed, such discourses should be taken into account by any moral theory that discusses musical activity—especially regarding music in Christian communities.

In this chapter, I have argued that musical meaning is established by shared experiences of embodied emotional orientation. That is, that music forms communities through its ability to marshal—to elicit, express, or mimic—human emotions and orient emotional postures toward or against ideas or objects or others. We encounter and experience the embodied emotions and feelings of ourselves and others in profound ways through music; these ways have been explained through academic models such as contour theory, compound ritual entrainment, and others. Encounters with and experiences of others' emotions influence our thinking, and when taken together with the argument of Chapter 2 read through the lens of Nussbaum's theorizations, suggest that music is a site where meaning and emotion intersect; reason and feeling converge in human bodies in musical activity. This affective intersection is intensely formational, as music forms affective communities, and when Smith's argument that we are formed most profoundly by what we love and desire is considered, it becomes clear that music plays an important role in the formation of both reason and relationships.

If stopped here, this account comes perilously close to circular reasoning: music is meaningful because it engages emotions, and it is emotional because it is meaningful. On one hand, I could say that cause and effect is simply too limited to account for the reality of human interactions with musical activity, yet this would be a profoundly unsatisfactory conclusion for an academic book! On another hand, and this is the hand I am playing, when confronted with a circular argument a researcher must look elsewhere for a conclusion: What does this convergence of meaning and emotion point to? *It points to the fundamental ontology of relationship for musical activity.*

Yet there is more to this analysis. As has been alluded to at several points in the preceding chapters, the value of *authenticity* contributes greatly to ethical understandings of music in Christian communities: music is "the only medium where people authentically express emotions"; music is good when it "expresses authentic emotions." What does "authentic" mean here, and how does this value of authenticity contribute to this discussion of music and ethics? The exchange between Heather and Lacey in Chapter 1 sheds light on this question, demonstrating how the value of authenticity is understood by negation: worship music was bad when it was "fakey" and manipulative. Setting authenticity and "fakey" as antonyms reveals that truthfulness forms the basis of emotional goodness in musical worship, but this realization does not clarify how authenticity solves the problem of oppositional communities as considered in Chapter 1.

Where discourse and formation collide—and indeed counteract each other—is in the valuation of the individual and where the locus of authenticity is placed: discourse necessitates the truthful participation of the individual in the linguistic negotiation of shared values and convictions—social good; formation necessitates the submission of the individual's linguistic negotiation out of the conviction that such a submission to the community will impel personal character development. While the individual authenticity of discourse may serve to work against the hegemony of con-formation, it can also become the impulse for relational rupture and "worship war."

Invoking the work of Cavell again, Kim's reflection from earlier in this chapter on the vulnerability of musical worship hinges on an understanding of authenticity cum goodness: if she sings or leads well—"authentically" or "good"—then she is exposed, vulnerable. Others can see and hear her affections, her bodily expressions of value and conviction. Formation ethics urges worship leaders into a narrative; the resulting performance is good when it exposes the leader, yet bad when it does not. Being exposed invites attack from those who disagree—with the gesture, the meaning, the genre, the affect, and so on—especially if the narrative is not engaged in an "orthodox" manner.

This is the problem of authenticity as a criterion of musical goodness: it demands both discourse and formation, which have often been constructed to counteract each other in real life. If music depends on honesty for its efficacy, and honesty requires vulnerability, then good music requires vulnerable participation (cf. Rommen's observations about truthfulness from Chapter 1). Failing to account for the way that music gives meaning to emotion and feeling to reason facilitates abusive expectations of vulnerable encounters with others in Christian communities because of the basic impulse of human beings to control others that Cavell draws out in *The Claim of Reason*.

What this reality points to is the same reality that the circular logic of musical meaning and emotion illuminate: that human beings are fundamentally relational. The bright side of this reality is that our desire is to join others in mutually agreed on forms of meaningful and feelingful musicking. The shadow side of this reality is that the need to control others often leads to an application of the concept of "orthodoxy" in the service of this controlling impulse—often under the guise ensuring Christian formation. What is needed for an account of music's ethical significance is a theory that takes this relational ontology as primary, affording space for meaning and affect, discourse and formation, individual and community, to be acknowledged and affirmed, constructed and celebrated, preserved and protected.

PART II

CARE, JUSTICE, AND BEING FOR OTHERS

A Proposal

3
Restore
Care, Justice, Relationships, and Music

Music's way of being in the world is inherently relational. To riff on John Blacking's (1974) classic definition, music is *relationally* ordered sound. Because of this reality, an ethical theory that gives a holistic account of human relationships is needed to understand music's ethical significance. I have argued that music's relational ontology can be understood in two ways; first, in Chapter 1, music is shown as imbued with meaning around which people build communities of agreement. Second, in Chapter 2, music is shown to be an affective activity that engenders emotional responses in its participants who in turn form social imaginaries and memories that are embodied through musical activity. I further argued that these two limbs of music's relational way of being in the world are not separated in lived reality but rather that meaning and emotion converge in human bodies through musical activity. This convergence is particularly potent in Christian communities.

Concurrent with my examination of music's meaning-making and affective community formation, I applied the ethical theories of discourse ethics and liturgical character formation ethics as analytical lenses for my fieldwork and theoretical developments, and I concluded that each is helpful but ultimately insufficient. In Chapter 1, I argued that Habermasian and Rawlsian discourse ethics as applied to church and worship music by Rommen (2007) and Porter (2016) provides a valuable frame for understanding how musical meaning is made and received, but alone it is not a sufficient means of understanding church music's ethical significance. Because musical meaning is even more unstable than linguistic meaning, discourse ethics alone was unable to offer a means of evaluating the goodness of musical meanings or of opposing divisively oriented communities from going to worship war with others who found that the musical sounds in these communities had different meanings or the musical meanings had different values. In Chapter 2, I argued that liturgical character formation ethics as described by Smith (2009), Hauerwas (1979, 2015), Saliers (1979, 1998) and others offers

Music for Others. Nathan Myrick, Oxford University Press (2021). © Oxford University Press.
DOI: 10.1093/oso/9780197550625.003.0004

important keys to understanding how musical worship's affective aspects shape individual and communal character, but the reliance of these authors on linguistic meaning similarly limited the application of their theories to musical activity. Moreover, many liturgical character formation ethicists assume a deterministic outcome for character formation based on adherence to doctrinal orthodoxy; in other words, they posit that if worship or music has a proper relationship to "orthodox" theology, then good ethical character will be formed.

Music's affective ontology ultimately questions the causality of "good" theology, as character formation ethics does not provide a sufficient means of evaluating the goodness of those associations or the theologies that inform them. Instead, the diffuse nature of musical meanings coupled with the uncontrollability of emotive responses to musical activity that in turn inform those meanings profoundly troubles deterministic character formation through musical worship while simultaneously revealing human need to control others. Furthermore, the criterion of truthfulness, or "authenticity," necessitates a vulnerable encounter with others where relational harm is often unintentionally inflicted during musical activity because of this need to control. Neither discourse nor formation ethics alone offers a suitable means of addressing such harmful musical activity.

In this chapter, I argue that feminist care-based ethics affords a fruitful way of holding together both music's relational meaning and its affective power while also offering a way of evaluating the actual goodness of the communities and identities formed in response to musical activity in Christian worship. Care ethics' assumption of relationships as ontological for human beings is a crucial point of convergence with music, defined here as an inherently, inescapably relational activity. As such, care ethics' purpose of enabling and supporting flourishing relationships points to a robust and holistic means of evaluating musical activities' ethical significance—especially in religious rituals. Further, its emphasis on attentiveness and responsiveness to the needs of the other in a timely and appropriate manner provides a way of understanding how musical worship can function ethically in discrete congregations. Care-based ethics provides a way of getting at the ethical dimension of music that neither reduces nor glamorizes its affective and subjective aspects while simultaneously acknowledging the ways that meaning and reasoning is engendered in musical action. In its more developed forms (see, for example, Farley [2002], Held [2006], and especially Nussbaum [2011]), care-based ethics emphasizes reciprocity, acknowledging the differences and agentive capabilities of the other and working toward the flourishing of others in a concrete and timely manner that is simultaneously discursive and formational; in this way it casts a vision of what caring musical ethics can accomplish and be.

However, I also argue that care ethics itself is incomplete; in its nascent forms especially (Gilligan 1982; Noddings 1984), an emphasis on relationships and care for intimates precluded concerns for justice. Despite the assertions of Held and others that care and justice are compatible and inform each other in important ways, the conflicts between claims of care and claims of justice are not easily resolved. In response to this conflict, I draw on the work of Howard Zehr (1990), John Braithwaite (2002), and others, to argue that if justice is oriented toward restoration rather than retribution, then the conflict between care and justice may be lessened to a great degree. As my fieldwork at Lakeshore suggests, however, this goal is still difficult to attain in real life.

Based on my observations and interviews coupled with the work of feminist ethicists along with philosophical musicologists Marcel Cobussen and Nanette Nielsen (2012), I argue that the ethical significance of musical activity may best be understood as care oriented toward restorative justice. By this I mean a responsive, reciprocal, and restorative posture toward relationships both near and distant that acknowledges the contributions and capabilities of each as agents within systems of power, directing relational affections toward restorative justice. To be sure, music can be used as a powerful source of rupture and control, but this does nothing to diminish the legitimacy of my claim; rather, it provides strong support for it. If music were used for restorative ends only, it would have no need of ethical evaluation, and this book would merely be an affirmation of music's inherent goodness. Instead, congregational music is *unethical when it is uncaring*, that is, when it is performed in a manner that fails to pay attention to the honest, relational needs of persons of varying positions of power in view of justice. In this frame, ethical music is music that preserves people in and restores people to just relationships with each other.

Aural Relationships: Music and the Other

My argument for care-based ethics in musical activity builds on the work of Marcel Cobussen and Nanette Nielsen, who, in their 2012 work *Music and*

Ethics, seek to "unravel 'ethical moments' which involve both ethical issues that warrant musical discussion and . . . musics that invite ethical explication" (1). Describing musical activity as a space where ethics happens, they argue for an "aural ethics." Such an aural ethics requires a radical hospitality to the musical other. They suggest that music metaphorically affords a deep world of hospitality; music consistently refuses to reduce the other to the same by virtue of its inherent need for differentiation, one note is not another—and cannot be for music to exist. Such inherent otherness provides both physical and metaphorical space for the human other to exist in shared musical space—a hospitality of/through music.

As Cobussen and Nielsen put it, music not only represents ethical values; through music, ethics sets itself to work (17, 34). An ethics of music implies a strategy of attentive listening that seeks to preserve both the space for and voice of the other. However, such an ethics cannot be understood as being relegated to the "metaphysics of morals, [as] music's call for an affective ethicality, resulting from a premediated contact with sounds, is dependent on bodily experiences and perceptions" (165). This ethic is not constructed upon a predetermined set of principles but rather has a single principle of an experience of musicking that is attentive to other performers, listeners, and composers. Using the metaphor of improvisation to describe how this hospitality goes beyond listening yet inextricably requires it, Cobussen and Nielsen argue that listening is necessary for good decision making and evaluation, and in turn for hospitable experiences of others in musical activities (86–92). This experience begins with and ends with listening in hospitality (166).

Cobussen and Nielsen's argument about hospitable aural ethics has many points of resonance with my arguments about meaning and affect from Chapters 1 and 2: musical hospitality is an attitude that creates space between listeners and performers and composers where encounters can happen and values and convictions may be negotiated so as to form and affirm affective relationships. Further, the inherently relational nature of music is fundamental for any ethical composition about music and ethics, and that *good* encounter with the other in/through music—both metaphorically and physiologically—requires hospitality as the first theme. In this way, hospitality as a guiding principle begins to address the dilemma of vulnerability and authenticity in musical activity, in that a posture of openness and welcome to others seems to resolve the conflict presented at the end of Chapter 2. However, as Cobussen and Nielsen point out, such relational aspects of music themselves fall victim to prejudice and assumptive patterns of goodness, as the "worship wars" so vividly demonstrate.[1]

Hospitality, then, requires acknowledgment and affirmation of difference; negotiating values and convictions together with forming and strengthening affective relationships must work against the tendency to desire communities that are only ever in agreement. This point draws out two latent questions that need to be raised about an ethic of musical hospitality: How might we determine what musical hospitality is or could be beyond listening to other styles of music? Further, how might we ensure, or certainly failing that, suggest, that such musical hospitality is indeed ethical?

Surely, we may listen to other music with devious intentions, and opening the metaphor up beyond simply listening and into musical creation highlights this problem more acutely. For instance, while Cobussen and Nielsen's example of improvisation helps to thicken what they mean by "aural hospitality," in the sense that improvisation always requires attentiveness to the agency of other players and responsiveness to their gestures with an eye toward the generic and contextual expectations of the discrete musical activity, it also raises a potential problem: How is the negotiation of an individual's agency over or against another's determined to be ethical? What of the desires or expectations of a given performer of her co-improvisers—for instance, what happens if two improvisers in a jazz combo both feel it is their turn to solo at the same time? If these needs are unmet, will that deter or damage their relationships? While Cobussen and Nielsen's appeal to Jean Luc Nancy's argument that freedom only happens in community (87) serves to mitigate against this critique to some extent, the hospitality they describe (improvisation notwithstanding) encounters the same obstacles that hinder the usefulness of the other ethical theories examined in the preceding chapters: negotiation of personal values and convictions is a good description of *how* ethics happens (which is Cobussen and Nielsen's aim) but not of ethics itself. Can we say no more than that it is good for each to decide for himself or herself what "good" is?

While hospitality does provide a guide for how those negotiations of personal values and conviction may be ethical, it does not go far enough; how might notions of "hospitality" differ from culture to culture or genre to genre, or, thinking more specifically about music in Christian communities, from congregation to congregation? Cobussen and Nielsen derive their metaphor for hospitality from Western music theory—namely, how harmony occurs through a predetermined progression of hierarchically ordered triads (while acknowledging that other musical forms could afford different metaphors). Interrogating this metaphor, hospitality as a guiding principle for encountering the other in and through musical activity breaks down when power structures are considered; thinking especially of the dynamics of Western music, the privilege of I and V within a key and the ascribed power to their pitches and relationships can be read conversely as a metaphor for oppression of II/ii, III/iii, or VI/vi. Within congregational settings, this critique asks, "Whose voice are we listening to," or "Whose values and convictions do we honor should there be a conflict?"

Yet I do not wish to throw out hospitality as a useful category for theorizing about music and ethics. Indeed, hospitality—both in listening to and making music—is a helpful guiding principle for encountering the other's vulnerability. Instead, I wish to scale back the metaphor and build on where it ceases to be effective by suggesting that there is an ethical theory that accounts for these problems of values and power and offers a concrete way of addressing them: feminist care ethics. Where the metaphor of hospitality suggests attentiveness to real difference between individuals and communities, care-based ethics insists on both attentiveness *and* reciprocity; where hospitality assumes relationships as a goal, care assumes relationships as ontological; where hospitality implies welcome but often stops there, care implies active engagement on behalf of the well-being of the other. Where hospitality seeks to preserve the interpersonal agency of others in small-scale social situations, care works to ensure that the agency of the other is able to flourish in full view of spectrums of power and oppression that may not be accounted for in the act of hospitality.

Care: Responsive, Reciprocal, and Restorative

Care-based ethics provides a helpful way of accounting for the relational ontology of human life. The concept of "care ethics" was first articulated in Carol Gilligan's landmark 1982 monograph, *In a Different Voice*. In this "little book that started a revolution," Gilligan argued, in contradistinction to the prevailing theories of moral development of her day that tended to skew toward indicating a lack of moral development in a majority of women, that women operate in a different mode of moral reasoning. This mode of moral reasoning takes relationships to be ontological, and through a series of selected interviews with women, Gilligan argues that women's moral reasoning is not inferior to that of men (as she contended developmental models had indicated) but is rather relationally—instead of objectively—oriented. As such, women were more inclined to consider the health of a relationship over and above objective fairness and adherence to rules. Thus, Gilligan's ethic of care centered around the development of moral reasoning that understood relationship and responsibility as the most important ethical impulses for women (1991, 16–23, esp. 19).

Building on the foundation laid by Gilligan, Nel Noddings's 1984 book, *Caring: A Relational Approach to Ethics and Moral Education*, articulated an explicit ethical theory derived from the experience of mothering. Noddings suggested that in the same way the care of a mother ("the one caring") for her child is focused on the well-being of the child, so an ethic of caring is concerned with the well-being of the "cared for" person who is in immediate relational proximity to the one caring. While Noddings regards motherly care as a natural state, she considers ethical caring a learned skill that involves intentionally recognizing who the one caring is caring for or is responsible to. In this frame, only living beings can be cared for as a person cannot care about ideas in the same way that she can care about people (although she does consider care for the environment a critical concern).

Noddings argued for a non-principled, non-religious, non-rule-based ethics of care based on the primary relational affections (in other words, desires and loves) of humans. This ethics of care is founded on a value of concrete relationships rather than abstract principles, such that an ethics of care may at times be forced to violate the principles of rights or rules in the pursuit of "good." This concrete foundation is the "ontology of relation," by which Noddings means that all ethical responses begin with a relationship of one to "an-other" (1984, 23–29).

Gilligan and Noddings contribute much to our understanding of relationships and responsibility as central to ethical concerns. However, their work is also deeply problematic for many ethical theorists. For instance, beyond an insistence on essential gender differences in moral reasoning, Gilligan's claim that women's primary mode of moral reasoning is singular (if complex) is deeply troubling in that it can silence the voices of women who, by virtue of other commitments (such as religious or vocational), might employ a different mode of moral reasoning or arrive at different conclusions arising from an orientation toward care.

Gilligan's construction of care ethics is helpful and valuable in raising to the surface the notion of "care" as a primary mode of moral reasoning, yet it is limited and even problematic in its method and claims. Gilligan seemed not to recognize the relevance of justice to care. I am not alone in these critical observations. Marilyn Friedman pointed out that even intimate relationships need justice and equity ("giving people their due [and] treating them appropriately," 66) in order for them to be truly caring (Friedman 1995, 61–78).[2] Further, Gilligan replicated the gender-essentialist model, and even in the best light, Gilligan's approach is "bimodal," affirming bifurcated forms of reasoning that link men, abstraction, and rights, on the one hand, and women, concretion, and relationships, on the other (Moody-Adams 1991, 195–212). This in turn is troubling in its assumption of (1) the moral superiority of one gender over another (irrespective of other contingent factors, such as race and socioeconomic status) and (2) essential gender differences.

Further, Noddings's elaboration of feminist care ethics has been critiqued on the grounds of her eschewal of justice. Sarah Lucia Hoagland expressed difficulty with Noddings's apparent preference for unequal relationships wherein the one-caring is in an "authorized" (authority) position over the cared-for (1991, 246–264). Hoagland and others take issue with Noddings's explicit refusal to acknowledge charges of injustice against her intimates, most gallingly in the (hopefully fictitious) example of being unable to physically oppose her racist family members in an imaginary conflict over racial equality; in this anecdote, she claims she would fight on behalf of what she believed to be injustice (that is, not giving each person their due; actively privileging one person over another) if her intimates were on that side (Noddings 1984 [2013], 108–113).

Commitments to relational care often conflict with commitments to justice: there are often disagreements between individuals within a given community or among several such communities over which of these commitments should predominate. In such cases, individuals and communities as a whole may be forced to choose between the values espoused by care and those espoused by justice. Lakeshore underwent just such a conflict during my study of that community. The narrative of their experience will draw this tension and conflict out into the open for better and clearer analysis of the problem.

Relational Rupture: Care versus Justice in Congregational Life

The conflict between care and justice is widespread and manifest in concrete events, and Christian communities are by no means immune to this reality; instead, they are often sites of highly visible and identifiable conflicts that can helpfully be framed as between commitments to relational care and commitments to a certain understanding of justice. During my time at Lakeshore, one such event illustrates this point profoundly. On November 30, 2016, Lake Shore Baptist Church voted by an 86 percent majority to adopt an official statement of affirmation toward members of the LGBTQ+ community. This vote took place during a Wednesday night supper and business meeting held at the church's building and had been preceded by a five-week series of seminars outlining the details and debates surrounding the question of whether queer-identifying persons should be affirmed or merely welcomed. These seminars included stories from several Lakeshore members who identified as LGBTQ+ or whose children so identified. Even prior to this series, the mostly elderly, middle-class, well-educated congregation "practiced affirmation" of queer persons by welcoming them to hold leadership positions in the church. The most prominent question in the minds of many was why a public statement was needed: If the church was already affirming, why make a big deal about it with a statement—especially when it might have negative repercussions in the highly "conservative" city of Waco, in central Texas, as well as among more conservative congregations in Lakeshore's Baptist networks? Despite these concerns, the overwhelming response of the congregation was in favor of the statement, and many who voted against it did so not because they opposed affirming queer persons but rather because they did not see the need for a public statement that would result in a social and ecclesial backlash that would likely sever many of those relationships.

As might be expected—and was indeed anticipated—the adoption of an affirming statement by a Baptist church in Waco made immediate waves. Despite Lakeshore's reputation as a progressive congregation on issues of race and gender (it was among the first Baptist churches in Texas to racially integrate in 1967 and ordain and appoint female pastors, in 1975 and 1985, respectively), a public declaration affirming LGBTQ+ persons was too much for many in Baptist life. Retribution was swift. Within two months the BGCT had removed Lakeshore from its fellowship (Lakeshore's senior pastor, Kyndall Rothaus, was not allowed to speak at the assembly that voted on the church's removal), and numerous op-eds and letters to the editor were published in local and regional Baptist publications bemoaning the loss of another congregation to the "liberal agenda." Despite overwhelming congregational support for the affirming statement, several prominent and long-tenured members of Lakeshore left the church in the wake of its ratification.

The results of these events can best be described as relational rupture. The loss of fellowship with the BGCT and other local Baptist congregations created rupture on both large and small scales: the church's relationships with other congregations and denominational institutions were severed, and the departure of some longtime friends and associates resulted in personal relational loss. Given Lakeshore's traditional values of hospitality, inclusion, and justice, the most prominent question for many members remained, How or can (or *should*) Lakeshore repair those relationships?

Many Christian communities, like communities of other sorts, deal with relational rupture and repair on a regular basis. Indeed, many Christian communities confess their purpose as one of restoring people to just relationships with each other, and ultimately with God. Yet in myriad and profound ways communities such as Lakeshore find themselves in tension with this *telos*, as relational restoration in one context seems to demand rupture in another. On one hand, commitment to full inclusion of all in the community is both a just and caring action, yet on the other, it is also one of rupture with personal friends and a broader network of congregations—perhaps just from the dominant perspective of the congregation but at the expense of relationship with those whom they will no longer be in a position to influence. It may indeed be argued that such relationships are no longer worth the effort needed to maintain them: Why should Lakeshore be troubled by the loss of ecclesial and personal relationships with those who do not agree with this application of one of its central beliefs and values? The answer to that question is both theological and pragmatic. In the first sense, the self-stated purpose of a community such as Lakeshore is to be, at the risk of redundancy, a fully inclusive relational community: "all are welcome," is the common refrain from the pulpit. For many, this means actively seeking to make and keep relationships within the congregation—even those who disagree about what "all are welcome" means. However, this kind of theological response is in many ways insufficient when individual agency is considered, as those who left did so of their own accord and were not ostensibly forced out (although this assertion is contested by at least one former member). On the other hand, relational rupture often precludes and eliminates discourse beyond polemics and strawmen. If relationships are continually sacrificed and discourse abandoned for the cause of justice (or rights, or orthodoxy, for that matter), then cycles of fracture and destructive "othering" are perpetuated. In the same way that many may be reticent to excommunicate racist relatives or xenophobic family members, many at Lakeshore have no desire to cut ties with those who have shared their religious convictions and commitments—sometimes for fifty years or more. This is the tension that is insufficiently addressed by musical discourse and liturgical formation ethics.

Care and Justice in Dialogue

In recent years, several scholars have attempted to address this kind of conflict without abandoning either care, that is, relationships, or justice, that is, "rational action in accord with abstract principles" (Held 2006, 62). A helpful development of care and justice is offered in Virginia Held's 2006 monograph *The Ethics of Care*. She frames the problem of care versus justice like this:

> To those focused on the values of care, it is apparent that if women, in their justifiable quest for equality, pursue justice at the expense of care, morality will suffer. For those previously engaged in care to become more and more like the free and equal, rational and unencumbered individuals of theories of justice will leave no one to nurture the relations of family and friendship, and to cultivate the ties of caring. To treat friends and family members as if relations between them were contractual bargains based on self-interest undermines mutuality and undercuts trust. (64)

In spite of this tension, care and justice are not always incompatible but are instead often complementary (69). However, Held's book is limited by the lack of a developed description of how care and justice integrate to support each other; for instance, while we may certainly have care without justice, Held does not offer the converse one would expect: that we cannot have justice without care (see Bagnoli (2006) for more on this). Indeed, she implies this but stops short of saying so. Instead, Held pivots and argues that her suggestion that care should form the meta context into which justice is set does not reduce justice, or rights, or even virtue to care but rather orients justice and virtues toward a relational morality (74–75).

Held's perspective on care and justice helps explain some of Lakeshore's narrative from an ethical perspective, in that publicly affirming the LGBTQ+ members of the congregation (i.e., assuring that they have full "rights," such as ordination or marriage) was both caring and just. However, it does not satisfactorily account for the relational rupture that resulted for those who believed that it was immoral for a Christian community to affirm LGBTQ+ persons in such a manner. Held's assertion that relationships are ontological for human beings supports her argument that care is the most basic form of morality (73), but her framework alone is unable to account for situations where relationships with some are upheld at the expense of relationships with others. At some point, care's assumptive power within relationships ends and the one cared for is free to make a choice about what is best for her (the "cared for"), what aligns with her values and convictions. This is one of the strengths of feminist theory, and while Held and others veer perilously close to the edge at times with evident assumptions of caring-from-on-high, so to speak, the insistence on acknowledging and respecting the agency of the other remains an important limit for ethical theorizing.

Held's suggestion that care forms the basis for justice begins to move closer to the interrelationship of care and justice I am arguing for as an ethic of musical activity. Yet this account of justice is still thin and will be helpfully thickened with a thoroughgoing account of human flourishing that frames both justice and care as constitutive of such flourishing.

Martha Nussbaum, writing about the methods used to evaluate human flourishing, suggests that any satisfactory account of care-and-justice-as-human-flourishing must be able to consider human potential as well as access to and attainment of goods that promote flourishing—what she calls "the Capabilities Approach," which she developed along with Amartya Sen (2002, 123–135; 2011, 18–20). Claiming that a moral theory based on assumptions of capabilities stemming from humanness affords a better means of social ordering and justice, Nussbaum's capabilities approach to feminist ethics includes the emphases of the other approaches yet marshals them in the service of fulfilling individual and social potential based on grounded circumstances and abilities. Against accounts based on measuring resources, preferences, and rights, an account based on capabilities is able to effectively measure flourishing for individuals and societies in ways the others cannot by allowing for individualized contextualizations of resources within broader social settings. Beginning from the question, "What is she actually able to do and be?" Nussbaum argues that there are ten "Central Capabilities" that must be "secured" for human beings to minimally flourish: Life; Bodily Health; Bodily Integrity; Sense, Imagination, and Thought; Emotions; Practical Reason; Affiliation; Other Species; Play; and Control over One's Own Environment (2011, 33–34).[3] Nussbaum's work supplies a broadly applicable theory of human flourishing from which to construct an account of caring and just music that does not fall victim to critiques of particularity and exclusiveness yet preserves the integrity of each agent as an individual by emphasizing compassion, respect, and contextualized individual capabilities.[4]

Influenced by Cobussen and Nielsen, Held, Nussbaum, and others, the musical care ethics I propose begins to take shape. From its inception, care ethics is concerned with particular individuals and relationships. Moreover, it takes emotions seriously as aspects of the whole human person, not as inhibitions to moral development. As I argued in the previous chapters, music is an inescapably relational activity that is both discursive, that is, it is interpreted to meaningfully convey values and convictions, and formational, that is, through the negotiation of these values and convictions identities and communities are constructed. Crucially, this discursive formation is affectively and emotionally constituted; it both *means* and *feels*, is both *rational* and *emotional*. In short, *musical activities embody the convergence of the tenets of moral theories of care*. Building on this foundation, and integrating the work of Nussbaum in particular, musical activity is ethical when it cares, that is, when it contributes to human well-being and flourishing.

The idea that music can contribute to human flourishing was illuminated in a number of ways by my conversation partners. In response to my questions—"Does music influence your sense of well-being?" and "Can music heal?"—the overwhelming responses were affirmative, yet nuanced. While nearly all of them affirmed the ability of music to influence their own personal well-being, many also noted that music's influences on well-being were intimately tied into human relationships with others. For example, Carin, from Harris creek, affirmed that music influenced her sense of well-being: "Yeah. Absolutely. Yeah." She described how music can cheer her up when she's "in a blah mood" or how "dance music" can motivate her to "clean her house" (an aspect of Nussbaum's Capability 4; cf. Hesmondhalgh [2013, 19]). She further noted that it influences her relationship with her husband. Crucially, she connected music's ability to heal directly to that relationship, noting that when her husband listens to "country music" he is reminded of his love for her and that in turn impels him to affirm their relationship through demonstrations of affection ("hugs and kisses"), which she understood as healing.

Speaking specifically of church music, Bob from Lakeshore said that the act of singing together with other people helped him reconcile his relationships with them: "If there's somebody in the congregation or choir that's singing by you that you may be angry at or don't like as much, when you're singing, all of that melts away." I asked if those feelings came back later, after the music was over, and he said that if they did they were "greatly watered down."

However, music did not always soothe or restore relationships; sometimes the relationships influenced the efficacy of music to "soothe [the] soul." For example, Reggie, a musician from Greater Ebenezer in his early sixties who answered my first question by inflecting music's ability to influence his well-being ("soothes my soul"), pointed out with an economy of words how relationship is vital in whether music influences his well-being. When asked if music influenced his sense of well-being, he responded, "It depends on where I'm at and who I'm with." Others emphatically denied that music positively influences their sense of well-being at church, although they affirmed that it did in other settings.

Two points can be derived from these reflections. First, for many, musical activity's influence on their sense of well-being was initially tied to their emotional responses to it. Often, as Reggie's response demonstrates, music's way of being in the world is to influence emotions that in turn contribute to a sense of well-being. Second, this emotional well-being was often tied to relationships with others. While my asking about healing right after asking about well-being may have influenced the answers I received to that question, it is telling that the healing was construed in relational terms that were integrated with emotional responses to music—either because of how music can inspire positive affections for family members and calm anger toward fellow congregants or of how it can invoke negative emotions toward others who are perceived as having violated or hurt them.

The negative aspects of music's relationship to well-being can trouble overly optimistic accounts of music that imply that music always contributes to human flourishing by forcing an acknowledgment of the ways that music can hinder that flourishing as well. Hesmondhalgh agrees; his is a *critical* defense of music because he also notes this tendency (2013, 3). This potential for harm points to the need for musical activity to be evaluated ethically, and it also points to how that may be done without falling into the regulative traps of *moralism* or *autonomism* that Cobussen and Nielsen identify: care that enables human flourishing as Nussbaum describes it. Evaluating musical activities from the perspective of discourse and formation go part of the way there, but they provide only an isolated interval of pitches; care toward justice-as-human-flourishing provides the tonic pitch in the chord as it orients the meaningful and affective relational aspects of musical activity toward care for the well-being of the other.[5] Indeed, musical practices in ecclesial settings often demonstrate the need for such an evaluative frame, as relationships are ruptured there as often as and perhaps more profoundly than in other spheres of life.

Musical care can move the conversation into fruitful territory by foregrounding the importance of relationships where both discourse and formation place the emphasis on the individuated self. This relational inflection affords important insight when considered through the lens of music's metaphor of relationships, illuminating the inescapable fact that relational health is at the center of human flourishing (fulfilling sense, imagination, and thought; emotions; practical reasoning; and play as well as affiliation in Nussbaum's list, expanding on Hesmondhalgh (2013), 19–20). Because music contributes to human flourishing through relationships, care-based ethics can be fruitfully employed to understand church music's ethical significance if oriented toward justice that repairs relational rupture rather than ignoring or accentuating it.

However, this account of justice-as-human-flourishing does not yet provide a means of naming and addressing the causes of relational rupture that inhibit human flourishing. While Nussbaum notes that violating the Central Capabilities of another is by definition injustice, we can and must say more about how efforts to enable flourishing through music can work against injustice beyond defining it. Justice, read through the lens of care, must also have a *restorative* orientation; when tempered and limited by attentiveness to the agency of others, caring musical worship works to repair relational rupture by restoring people to just, that is, flourishing, relationships with each other.

Restorative Justice

Care and justice, as Held, Farley (2002), Nussbaum, and others have contended, read and interpret the other as the pursuits in which each is engaged; people who care seek justice for their intimates when they are the victims of oppression, but they also recognize that justice makes claims on the activities of those intimate relations. It would be a grave mistake to refuse to acknowledge that unjust actions occur with great regularity in relationships (both intimate and distant) the world over. The accounts of care considered here suggest that the pursuit of justice-as-human-flourishing is equivalent to what has been called "restorative justice" by Howard Zehr, John Braithwaite, Carolyn Boyes-Watson, and others. According to the model of restorative justice, the goal of justice is to restore both the victims and oppressors to flourishing human relationships, if not with each other, then certainly with others.[6] The editors of the *Handbook of Restorative Justice* (2013) describe restorative justice like this: "approaches designed to make wrongdoers aware of the nature and magnitude of the harm they caused to other people and of their obligation to atone for that harm through constructive and reparative gestures and deeds." Further, this approach is designed to "pave the way to forgiveness and reconciliation, the reintegration of wrongdoers into the community and the healing of victims' trauma" (2013, xxi).

Thinking with Held and Nussbaum suggests that relationships need to be healthy in particular ways.[7] It then becomes clear that an absence of an account of justice damns any attempt at constructing ethics around the maintenance of relationships alone. Yet taken together with this description of restorative justice, their work indicates that care—that is, ethics beginning with the ontology of relationships—needs an orientation for naming and opposing injustice that seeks to preserve the health of those relationships. Indeed, restorative justice provides the basis on which a relationship may be repaired. When considered through the lens of restorative versus retributive justice, the one caring may understand justice as being marshaled in the service of care; as restoring relationships and facilitating the realization of others' capabilities.

This account of just caring or caring through justice finds a voice in the affective and discursive activities of its proponents. Indeed, the notion of *voices*—both amplified and silenced—has great import for any consideration of human flourishing and agency. Moreover, listening and speaking *to* others is an important prelude to advocating on behalf of others; acknowledging the voice of another and that person's capability to leverage that voice is crucial to an ethic of care that marshals itself for just ends while pursuing justice in the service of care.

Musical Caring

It is now time to fashion the materials I have been assembling over the course of this book into a theoretical means of evaluating both the impact of music in Christian communities on ethical reason and action and the impact of music on moral thought in general. The care ethics that I have described provides a powerful heuristic tool for evaluating the goodness of music that does not exclude its capabilities for care nor confine it to pre-determined courses of conduct. Jeff R. Warren (2014) has argued that music places us in relationships that require responsiveness of varying degrees. I suggest that the nature of this responsibility is to care for the well-being of others, both distant and proximate. This care involves attentiveness: observing, listening to, and talking with others in order to identify their capabilities and desires. Attentiveness is additionally composed of an orientation and posture of agentive acknowledgment, both of the self and the other; it requires being aware of the power dynamics at work in the relationship and orienting the self toward the best case of each party. Inasmuch as caring values relational harmony and health, attentiveness presupposes reciprocity within the frame of capability; each responds to the other as each is able. An important part of musical care is preserving the agency of the other; this involves making sure that space is made for the other to be received and acknowledged—inclusive of their differences—in a hospitable way, as Cobussen and Nielsen argue. This necessarily takes into account positions and dynamics of power, yet operates under an assumption of the equality of intrinsic human value and worth, such that persons in positions of power do not violate the agency of others through music, as this would be an unjust act.

Congregational music, then, is ethical when it enables human flourishing for each individual in the community; when it provides space for people to voice their needs to each other and to God honestly—without fear of reprisal if that expression fails to resonate with the convictions of those who may wield greater power in a given community (Nussbaum's Capability 4); when it affords people space to sing with each other and experience emotions—both joyful and remorseful—without denying or discounting them or manipulating them to gain influence or leverage (Capability 5); when it invites personal reflection and evaluation of assumptions (Capability 6); when it unites people in meaningful and feelingful (embodied memory of relationships and feelings, Dueck 2017, 117) relationships that celebrate the real differences that exist between them (Capability 7); when it brings enjoyment and rest for individuals (Capability 9). These ethical and caring aspects of musical activity are realized when they are directed toward preserving and maintaining the relational health of the community as individuals *and* community within a broader society. Further, it is ethical when it calls out injustice; when it names violations of human capabilities and acts of oppression. Finally, it is ethical when it does not abandon hope for reconciliation and restoration of ruptured relationships both within and beyond the bounds of the congregation. This does not mean emotionally coercing an abused woman to return to her alcoholic husband or an assaulted child to return to his violent mother. Instead, it means making every effort to make the husband or mother aware of the effects of their actions and move them toward well-being both as individuals and relationships. This hope may often go unrealized, but it cannot be abandoned despite the risk it will not come to fruition.

Taking these ideas together with my arguments from Chapter 1 and Chapter 2, I contend that a musical ethic of care is one that pays attention to the relational and affective discourses that music embodies and seeks simultaneously to leverage those powerful discourses toward human flourishing while acknowledging and preserving the agency of others who might not share in the perspectives and opinions of the self. It also pays attention to music's discursive capability to protest and embody justice in caring and restorative ways, declaring identity and humanity, on the one hand, and opposing injustice—that is, realities that prohibit flourishing, on the other. Moreover, musical care calls for a response to the declared needs and desires of the oppressed and victims of unjust action. This response may indeed be plural, as in certain situations the response may simply be to make music that identifies with the suffering or jubilation of the other or perhaps listening respectfully to the songs of the other, or it may perhaps encompass both. In any context, musically caring responses require attentiveness to the particularity of both that context and the individuals who populate it. Chapter 4 will look at how musical care might appear in the discrete Christian communities that this book refers to by engaging Christian theological ethics at length. In doing so, it clarifies the latent theological claims of relational ontology that have popped up at various points in this book and points to the reality of mutuality in just, healthy, human relationships.

4

Response

Music, Others, and God

Theological Ontology of Relationships

The preceding chapters have revealed something inherent to Christian traditions in North America—something that needs to be addressed. That something is the conflict between orthodoxy and ethics, between the two poles of goodness that are claimed by Christian communities. My contention is that the ontology of relationships commands primacy in theological reflection; when made primary, it resolves the tension between ethics and orthodoxy by demanding that each be caring and just—that is, that each contribute to human flourishing as Nussbaum describes it.

From a Christian theological perspective, the ability to respond ethically raises the question of God's agency in the world; human agents respond to the needs of others as they are able, but how they respond is determined by how they understand God's agency in the world. Thinking with James Gustafson and Dietrich Bonhoeffer in particular, I argue that the claim of Matthew 22 and 24–25 is that a Christian ethical response of caring justice is an act of loving God and neighbor, and that in lived reality these things are symbiotic: "What you have done to the least of these you have done to me."

I begin with an engagement of Jeff R. Warren's (2014) musical responsibility ethics through the lens of my fieldwork. Putting his argument into conversations about the connection between music and responsibility that I had with my research participants, I both affirm and expand his theory by showing how responsibility may be invoked in musical worship, but I also show how the indefiniteness of the responsibility he proposes limits its effectiveness. However, Warren's theory can be fruitfully taken further by adding "to care justly" to his formulation without scaling back the scope of his claim. I then develop the theological impulses that have remained largely latent in this book thus far, showing how my extension of Warren's claims finds theological support while simultaneously contributing to theological conversations in its own right.

Music for Others. Nathan Myrick, Oxford University Press (2021). © Oxford University Press.
DOI: 10.1093/oso/9780197550625.003.0005

"What Would That Even Look Like?" Relational Response Ethics in Christian Communities

"What does music do in church?" *I asked Kevin, a Fuller student and pastor of a multicultural evangelical church in Hollywood. He initially responded as many other Christian leaders had done:*

> It helps my ministry by setting the mood. It kinda sets the tone of, like—you know how I was talking about being under the influence of that song, or music? We do that collectively at our church. It's like that music allows us to forget about everything, it encourages us to forget about everything and be present to, what we call, "the Spirit of God." And I think that there's also the element of being responsive to God. Right?

Kevin had earlier spoken of music's ability to present "truth" in emotionally applicable ways, connecting people to each other through this truth, and his answer assumes my knowledge of that aspect. I then asked him if music made people responsible for each other. His face registered a flicker of something, perhaps surprise, as he reflected. Then he repeated the question: "Responsive to other people?" "Yeah, like in worship at church," *I clarified. He paused, staring out the windshield as we made our way through the downtown traffic, and responded as though thinking out loud,*

> Bro, you know that's interesting. I just realized that a lot of times it can be kind of individualistic in a sense. Like you close your eyes and you raise up your hands and stuff. But I don't think I've ever thought of it as a response to other members in our church. And I wonder what that would look like. Like, um, [pause] wow. That's interesting.

"Do you think it should be?" I queried. He answered enthusiastically,

> Yeah! Yeah, that'd be really, that'd be really great. Like I said, I wonder what it's like, [pause] I wonder what that would look like.

Kevin continued reflecting on "what that would look like," noting that his church is primarily Korean American but also has some African American and Latinx members. He remembered that their worship leader abandoned the set list the week Philando Castille[1] *was shot and instead led the entire congregation in songs of lament. He further noted that this was particularly impactful, since he thought the majority of his congregation, being Korean Americans, did not experience "police brutality" in the same ways the African American members did. He asked again and again what it would look like to respond musically to the racial and political injustices that occur in our communities in real time. I confessed that I did not know and that my lack of knowledge was the impetus for my research. He pressed me,* "Like, 'I'm being more responsible to my neighbor, right?' " *I nodded. He thought for another moment and then talked through an example that came to mind.*

> Okay . . . You know what we did, we tried this one praise night thing, where we . . . played the same four chords again and again, drums playing and everything. And we asked each person to sing a couple lines, and as soon as they sang a couple lines we joined and repeated their thing. And we only had seven or eight people show up, but each person got a chance to sing a line, and we echoed that line. I remember that was really powerful.

For the rest of our conversation, Kevin continued reflecting on the slow-dawning epiphany that church music could have profound significance for human relationships, noting that musical worship at his church was "kinda like a concert, honestly, many times. . . That bothers me! I didn't realize that would bother me until you asked me that question." "Sorry!" I *responded. He replied immediately by saying,*

> No, that's a good thing! And I think the songs should be contextualized to what we're singing what's bothering us in this country. I mean, what would it look like to react to what's going on with our current political administration, President Trump and everything, that bothers people, and either try to find worship music that reflects that, or maybe encourage them to write something of their own and share that together. That'd be interesting.

Response Ethics and Music

The theme of responsibility is an important, final element of the relational ethics I am arguing for in musical activity. Jeff R. Warren's *Music and Ethical Responsibility* (2014), provides a helpful point of departure for understanding how music can both invite and require an ethic of responsibility. Warren argues that musical experience necessarily involves encounters with others and that ethical responsibility arises from those encounters (1). He suggests that the phenomenological experience of music and other people in musical events and activities places limits on us that alter the way we experience music and consequently how we experience others. This is because music is inextricably linked to human relationships—even the inherent nature of music itself is relational, be it pitch, note, text, score, or other elements. Moreover, any activity of music involves others, whether encountered through physical presence or through such virtual means as history, memory, or imagination. Because of this relational aspect, ethical responsibilities to others should not be suspended in any musical endeavor. Instead, the activity of listening to and performing music with others causes us to enter into relational responsibility with them; "the relational leads to the ethical through responsibility, through the valuing of others, the limiting of ourselves for the sake of others, and giving, listening, responding to and respecting others—the improvisation of human relationships" (134). Following Emmanuel Levinas, Warren suggests that moral rules of a society should rest on ethical responsibilities of its individual members to one another. In this way, he parses the moral laws and rules of a given society and the ethics of responsibility that he is suggesting.[2]

Warren argues that music participates in ethical responsibility in two ways: first, that musical experience can respond to ethical responsibilities, and second, that music discloses ethical responsibilities (21). There are several aspects of Kevin's reflection over the course of our conversation that demonstrate how Warren's suggestion might look in a discrete context. First, Kevin's reflection demonstrates how music can disclose ethical responsibility; he noted that he often treated music as a tool with which to "set the mood" for his "ministry," by which he ostensibly meant the sermon. He then realized that if music "connects people" and offers them a means of "handling truth" in emotionally important ways, then understanding music as being solely about an individual encounter with "God" during musical worship—a common evangelical approach—was counterproductive. He further recognized that musical worship is both meaningful and emotional and is therefore capable of disclosing the gravitas of certain events or experiences to others in profound, self-formative ways, as suggested by his memory of musical worship the week Philando Castille was shot.

Second, he told of the prayer service where the band vamped over a short progression while individuals sang their prayers, after which the rest of the group repeated their prayers with them; this demonstrates how music can be an ethical response to events and situations. In providing affective space for each individual to give voice to personal needs and desires in concert with each other—being heard and joined in that prayer—the prayer service demonstrated how attentiveness, difference, and mutual respect can be engaged in musical worship.

The Trouble with Responsibility: Relating Selves and Others through Music

Warren's theory of relational responsibility in musical ethics was borne out in much of my fieldwork, as my conversation with Kevin exemplifies. Through observations of congregants during musical worship and discussions about the way church music functions within interpersonal relationships, several of Warren's core arguments were affirmed: relationships do indeed lie at the heart of musical activity (2014, 21–30)—especially in Christian worship; music is in itself intrinsically relational; musical meaning is negotiated with others, is bound up together with its affective reception, and is further configured in relation to affection and human relationships (143); human relationships are, in turn, evaluated and determined within "social imaginaries," which are in turn constructed out of the symbiotic elements of emotion and reason (135–163); emotion and reason converge in the human body during musical participation, thus music is ethically significant.

Warren's reluctance to provide what he terms a "hard and fast application" (187) for his theory is both necessary and limiting. On the one hand, a hard and fast "how to" manual for ethical musicking would be destined to failure because there are too many variables during musical activity for a manual to address. Books (such as this one) cease to evolve once they are published. On the other hand, it is exceedingly difficult to ascertain what "responsibility" entails in any given scenario of music phenomena.

For many, the most common response to the question of responsibility is equivocation. When I asked whether music made people feel responsible for others, most answered immediately in the affirmative—perhaps because they felt that music ideally *should* do so—but then they struggled to find reasons to support their affirmation. For instance, Dan, who, as a youth director from Harris Creek was indeed a church leader, responded with "That's a good question. . . . I think, in some ways . . . I don't know if I would have phrased it like that, but, I think in some ways [it does]." Carin, also from Harris Creek, had a similar reaction and, intriguingly, on pondering the question, related a change in perspective toward other worshippers: "I'm going to say, and I never thought of that question before, maybe makes me a little less judgmental. Maybe show them a little grace, maybe not expect them to be perfect [?]" Frida was an education professor from Greater Ebenezer who affirmed responsibility in musical worship in terms of being responsible for herself:

> I feel responsible for making sure that I'm receiving the word of God but also responsible that I'm being participatory and living my life where I can be an example to others because we all go [to] the church. We all have a responsibility to be in the presence of God and to take our own souls and then we go out.

Some were less affirming that music made them feel responsible for others. Reggie, a musician from Greater Ebenezer, said "Kinda, sorta," and framed his answer in terms of playing with another person in a band. He described how some musicians are better than others and that he feels less responsible for certain musicians when they make mistakes in performances. Reggie's answer was decidedly more negative when I asked about others in church: "I really don't worry about the other people. No. I mean when I'm singing, I mean, I'm in the spirit. So, whatever message that I sing out and feel [about or from] God is what I feel they experience."

Others, about one-third of my conversation partners, were more definite in their disagreement. CJ from Harris Creek said, "Nothing, well, no, not necessarily a responsibility for them as far as . . . in the moment." Kim also said, "I don't think it does because of boundaries. You know? Like, 'You're responsible for yourself.'" Dave, a middle-aged pastor from Arizona interviewed as part of the SXSW research, said, "It should. I don't know that it *does*."

These responses illuminate a central point of Warren's theory—that although people "should" be responsible to others in music, they often are not. Warren (2014) argues that human relationships are central to meaningful music experiences, that ethical responsibilities arise from such experiences, and that there are impediments to its effectiveness for invoking ethical responsibility in human relationships. These impediments are twofold: first is what Warren calls "the culture industry's" commodification of music (184). Second, this commodification of music leads to a fracture of human relationships in and around music and obscures the ethical responsibilities that arise from such relationships. Warren does not advocate the destruction of the culture industry; instead, he indicates that its presence is the reason for his book. Yet the "commoditization of music" is only one possible reason for many people's ambivalence about whether music necessarily entails responsibility.

Another possible reason, more immediately applicable to Christian communities, is the collision of commitments with individual and communal authenticity discussed at length in Chapter 2. This collision is often accentuated by practices of individualization of musical worship, particularly within North American Protestantism. This individualization has been identified by Martyn Percy as "an abrogation of the social" (1996, 286) and by Mark Labberton as "tromping in the spirit," by which he means intentional unawareness of others during musical worship (exemplified by a story of a worship leader who quite literally was tromping on the feet of other congregants because he was so engrossed in musical worship; 2008, 21). Indeed, many of the responses to my suggestion of responsibility through music were couched in terms of *personal* responsibility, which confirms part of the critique offered by scholars such as Percy and Labberton. The effect of an individualistic focus on worship as solely about a "personal relationship with Jesus" in evangelical churches often trumps social awareness or obligation ("[losing our] neighbor," as Labberton (2008) puts it, 20). As Warren (2014) argues, in order for people to understand the relational ethics of musical responsibility, they must first be alerted to its reality. In this way, Warren is not advocating a certain set of moral laws to govern the use and activity of music, but rather he is "making propaganda for a style of thinking" (188) about musical meaning and the ethical responsibility that arises from it.[3]

However, as I argued earlier, ascertaining what music means is not straightforward: what music means is symbiotic with how it feels, and how it feels is profoundly part of its relational ontology. This re-direction of Warren's claim, from meaning to affect, is illustrated by Dan, who in answering my question described the relational and emotional responsibilities he felt toward the family whose teenaged son had recently died: "When I [see them worshipping in church] there's definitely some inspiration [that] makes [me] want to connect outside of that moment as well." He later described how seeing the emotions that musical worship evoked or gave place to was integral to how his relationship went with them and how he understood the family's interpretation of "Before the Throne" (see Chapter 2).

Extending the emotional aspect of musical responsibility goes beyond seeing the emotion of others to having feelings of *one's own about others* in musical worship. Stan, a congregant from Lakeshore who affirmed feeling a sense of responsibility to others during musical worship, said in a follow-up Facebook Messenger conversation that this sense of responsibility is directed toward forming community affectively: "I really want people to pull together and [I] get frustrated when I can't/don't seem to [see any] impact on them/the performance." This perspective was more positively shared by Carin, who noted later in our conversation that she did experience a sense of responsibility for others during worship in relation to her bodily gestures, specifically, whether or not to raise her hands or move along with the music. Her concern was initially that she would be a distraction if she did raise her hands, but later she decided that her actions might encourage others to do the same and experience a fuller sense of God's presence in musical worship. This perspective is further clarified by Frida's qualified affirmation of individual responsibility to act obediently to God's working in her life as an example to others.

While congregational music is likely not the kind of music Warren had in mind when writing his book, examining his theories from the perspective that this specific musical activity affords helps to flesh them out and points to how they may work in real life. Importantly, my conversation partners were more than twice as likely to affirm that music gave them a sense of responsibility for others *in a congregational setting* than they were in general.[4] This is likely because personal relationships are more readily identifiable in a congregation than outside of one; church members are ostensibly committed to the relationships with others in the church, and therefore they experience responsibility for them through musical worship more readily than through non-congregational music.

Finally, part of the problem my interlocutors had in answering my question was the indefiniteness of what "responsibility" entailed. I crafted the question to be open-ended because Warren's argument for responsibility is similarly indefinite. Indeed, though Warren's suggestion is on the face of it correct, the relationship between music and responsibility to others needs to be pursued further. To provide a useful basis for an ethical framework for musical activity, two additional questions must be addressed: How are we responsible to each other in music or through music? And what are we responsible to do? In order to support my argument that we are responsible to care justly for the relational health of others, the theological underpinnings of this claim need to be explicated.

Theological Response Ethics: Agency, Care, and Power

> *And a lawyer asked him a question. . . . "Teacher, which commandment in the law is the greatest? He said to him, "'You shall love the* LORD *your God with all your heart, and with all your soul, and with all your mind.' And a second is like it: 'You shall love your neighbor as yourself.' On these two commandments hang all the law and all the prophets."* (Matthew 22:35b–40, NRSV)

My argument for care ethics oriented toward restorative justice in musical worship also has a theological dimension that, while implied at various points throughout this book, must now be explicated. Following many scholars of American Christian social ethics, my ethical proposal is grounded in the text of Matthew 22 cited above. I wish to situate my argument as a development of the response ethics proposed by H. Richard Niebuhr and James M. Gustafson in the late twentieth century in conversation with the work of Dietrich Bonhoeffer: namely, that care oriented toward restorative justice in music is a response to Jesus's interpretation of the greatest commandment. In other words, to love God with everything and your neighbor as yourself can be described as caring for them, and that Jesus's inclusion of the law and the prophets connects this caring to acts of justice.

Stanley Hauerwas, in his commentary on Matthew (2006), rhetorically asks how we may know what love is. In response, he argues that we are able to know what it is to love our neighbor and God because of our experience of God's love for us: "We love because God first loved us" (1 John 4:19). He goes on to argue that Jesus's invocation of the law and prophets keeps love from devolving into saccharine sentimentality (193–194).[5] While I affirm that justice checks care in the same way that Hauerwas suggests the law checks sentimental love, the thrust of my invocation of care is in an effort to temper Hauerwas's (and others') hard-mindedness toward the centrality of relationships in Christian ethics.

To exclude emotions as a potential basis for moral action is misguided and is a fool's errand when the arguments of Begbie (2011), Smith (2009), Nussbaum (2001, 2011), and indeed my own are considered. If we insist that love of others contains no trace of sentiment, then we deny ethical actors' full humanity by reducing them to a single aspect of their being. Nevertheless, sentiment alone cannot rule the day, for humans are not only the sum total of our sentiments but are rather the composites of the diverse, myriad ways of being human. Indeed, this is one of the many ways that musical activity discloses what it is to be human: that we are both emotional and sentient, rational and affectionate. Furthermore, for sacred music scholars, trying to ascertain musical meaning using only lyrical analysis in order to determine doctrinal orthodoxy can obscure what Smith (2009) points out in *Desiring the Kingdom*: that humans have a tendency to justify intellectually what they, in the first instance, love and desire.

Keeping in mind my intent to attenuate the anti-sentimental impulse within some theological and scholarly sacred music conversations, I turn now to theological considerations of response ethics that modify even as they agree with Warren's argument of music as invoking ethical responsibility: What kind of responsibility is invoked? Responsibility to do what?

The responsive tradition of American theological ethics dates back to at least the late nineteenth century and counts among its exemplars figures such as Walter Rauschenbusch, Reinhold and H. Richard Niebuhr, and a host of others. Situated geographically in North America and temporally in the twentieth and twenty-first centuries, these scholars have largely articulated Christian ethics as being responsive, that is, as responding to others and ultimately to God as one is able. For example, in *The Responsible Self*, H. Richard Niebuhr argues for a realistic mode of ethical action that is governed by an understanding of the self as being responsible to and for the well-being of those who are in community with it (1978, 69–72). Drawing on his brother Reinhold's ethic of realism in that it begins with an understanding of the self in relation to history (1955, 1971), H. Richard Niebuhr extends it to include the self's relationship to society and to God.

This essential recognition of relationship as the foundation for an ethic of appropriate responsibility is itself built on a recognition that the self is distinct from the other yet is in many ways realized as a self through encountering the other. Drawing on the work of Martin Buber, particularly his I-Thou/I-It construction of human relationships, Niebuhr posits that the idea of the human self is socially formed, in that the reflexive nature of self-inquiry is only possible inasmuch as the other is encountered. This other can be an agent (Thou) or an object (It). If it is an object, then the self does not have an inherent responsibility toward It, but if it is an agent, then responsibility is enacted in that the self has some semblance of a relationship to the Thou (1978, 72–76; cf. the discussion of music as moral agent in the Introduction).

In unpacking his understanding of responsibility, Niebuhr states that there are four elements to the theory of responsibility: *response*, *interpretation*, *anticipation*, and *social solidarity.* In response, our self-agency is recognized to be relationally conditioned by the actions of those around us (the I-Thou) so that each action is a response. This responsive action is necessarily constructed on an interpretation of the actions to which we are responding; interpretation is contingently modified by the anticipated response of the other to our action. Finally, action is responsible if an agent takes each of these elements into account together within the frame of social solidarity, in that a good response is necessarily determined by the community one inhabits (61–65). In this way, the encounter with the other in relationship is not only an I-Thou but is more importantly an I-You, in that the other is *known* within the standards of society; social moral laws are mutually constituted on the ethical principle of the response/interpretation/anticipation/solidarity cycle in such a way that the other is knowable, albeit in a limited way (78–79, cf. Cavell 1999 in Chapter 1).

Within such a postulation, the question of universal ethics, if not answered completely, is at least asked differently:

> And now in *cathékontic* ethics, or the ethics of fitting, we find ourselves led to the notion of universal responsibility, that is, of a life of response to actions which is always qualified by our interpretation of these actions as taking place in a *universe*, and by further understanding that there will be a response to our actions by representatives of universal community. (87–88).

Yet this ethical responsibility of fittingness is always engaged in a particular time and place, and our actions are configured in the liminal now in response to actions (both self's and other's) of the near and distant past in anticipation of the community's (of which the "I" is a part) future response (108–126). Niebuhr's use of "universal" here does not mean for all time and all places but rather is defined in relation to a larger social reality that is nonetheless still relationally constituted, as ethical responses are not merely the concern of the self. Moreover, the self is in a dependent relationship to the other, as we are not hermetically sealed individuals but are rather "members of one another."

James M. Gustafson continued this line of ethical reasoning in *Ethics from a Theocentric Perspective*, yet he differed from Niebuhr theologically in that Gustafson assumes less of an agentive position for God than does Niebuhr. Whereas Niebuhr understood God as an active agent in the world—acting with individuals in society and history—Gustafson locates "God" as the limitations of human agency, as "the forces that bear down on us and sustain us" (1981, 273–274). Instead of an ethics that understands God as an agent whose actions in history are to be responded to, interpreted, and anticipated in relational responsibility, Gustafson sees such responsibility being directed only toward human agents and material nature. His reasons for differing in this from Niebuhr are complex and nuanced, and Gustafson sees Niebuhr's doctrine of God as being too limited, on the one hand, and offering too much excuse for unethical human action, on the other (274 ff, for instance). Gustafson argued that the human agent's responsibility to the other and to the world is care for its well-being. Niebuhr argued that "responsibility says 'God is acting in all actions upon you. So, respond to all actions upon you as to respond to [God's] actions'" (1978, 126), whereas Gustafson argued that God *is* or *is in* the actions that act upon us (1981, 264). Within this frame, it becomes clear that responsibility to act on behalf of others is to act as to God: "What you have done to the least of these you have done to me" (Matthew 25:40, 45).

To return to Hauerwas's rhetorical question of how we know what love is, in light of both Niebuhr's and Gustafson's claims about the agency of humanity in response to constraint, it is not affirming the consequent to read Matthew 25:40 in reverse. In other words, if we know what love is and are able to love because of God's love for us, and our love is construed in active terms as Jesus says in Matthew 22, then when taken together with the reality of our actions toward others (loving or unloving) as being done to God, it becomes clear that we know what love is because we have been loved by other people. In the same way that what we do to others we do to Jesus, then in what others do to us is the way we experience Jesus. Yet even "they," the other, are as much a Thou as we are in the scope of Jesus's words. As I have argued in Chapter 2, this acknowledgment of the humanity of the other means that our loves and desires—our affections—are imbricated with our knowledge; we know what love is and how to love because we are loved by others as by God, and therefore we are able to reciprocate this love in response to the claims of Jesus.[6]

This double inversion of the I/Thou—Thou/I illustrates that reciprocal human relationships are the axle around which the wheel of response ethics turns. Yet it also illustrates that relationships cannot mean our intimates alone but must always again include attentiveness to those who might qualify as "the least of these," who may include us from time to time. There is a latent suggestion in the parallel narrative of the Greatest Commandment in Luke

10 that places the agency of loving actions into the hands of the "Thou" rather than the "I." As Robert Funk wrote in 1964, "as victims we are 'loved' by the enemy" (58). Like many of Jesus's parables, I find myself caught by misidentification with the characters of the story; I am likely as not the one in need of care and restoration from my own injustice.

When considered in light of this argument for directing our agentive orientation toward love of God through love of others, the problem of orthodoxy as I described it in Chapter 2 comes more clearly into focus. The syllogism that Cherry quotes—"Right worship (*orthodoxy* . . .) leads to right action (*orthopraxy*) which, in turn, leads to right affection (*orthocardia*)"—has ascribed a sequential, cause-and-effect relationship to concepts that are actually symbiotic: the active love and worship of God occurs *through* active love of neighbor. To riff on Gustafson, active love of God *is* or *is in* active love of neighbor. To take this one step further, which I cannot resist, any claim cannot be "orthodox" if it is not always also characterized by orthopraxis *and* orthocardia. I do not, *cannot*, love God without loving my neighbor—and accepting my neighbor's love for me.

Relational Theology: Grace and Being for Others

Taking Niebuhr and Gustafson together with Warren, I suggest that music invokes a theological responsibility to love others in concrete and practical ways as we are able; to care in appropriate and just ways that enable human flourishing as I described it in Chapter 3. However, this kind of care is costly as it may also involve appropriate acts of justice that transgress the bounds of personal comfort and safety. I ground this suggestion theologically in the work of Dietrich Bonhoeffer, who argued that ethical response to God's gracious love was to act on behalf of others, "being for others."

In his extended reflection on the "Sermon on the Mount" in Matthew, chapters 5 through 7, *Discipleship* (1937 [2001]), Bonhoeffer argues persuasively for an understanding of "costly grace" as that which is not "cheapened" by evil action (2001, 171–175). An acceptance of grace, Bonhoeffer argues, demands the sacrifice of one's own self-righteousness ("piety," 161). No more can the person who has encountered such radical grace consider anything about her or himself as worthy of it. This does not lead to an inactive faith of passivity for Bonhoeffer; instead, such costly grace frees the individual from the constraints of self-righteousness ("the law") and enables ethical action

(18). Freedom, defined as such, violates the rules of self-righteous "piety" and insists instead on something far more radical: a life of committed action on behalf of others (175).

In his unfinished and provocative manuscript, *Ethics* (1949 [2005]), Bonhoeffer continues this line of thought by claiming that a life of committed action on behalf of others is identified by its similarity to the life of Christ—"the man for others"—by living "for others" (2005, 432). This claim is further established by his insistence that acts of service to God must be bound up in acts of service to human beings in light of the incarnation. In Jesus, the God-human, the fullness of sacred reality was revealed in profane form (59).[7] For Bonhoeffer, the distinction between sacred and profane action is obliterated in Christ, and so all action can be engaged as an act of loving God.

Emmanuel Levinas contributes a relational theory of existence to the discussion from an ethical perspective outside Christian theology. Levinas (upon whose work Warren, Rommen, and Cobussen and Nielsen build their theories), in his book *Entre Nous: Thinking of the Other*, suggests that "when human existence interrupts and goes beyond its efforts to *be* . . . there is a vocation of an existing-for-the-other stronger than the threat of death [italics mine]" (1998, xii). Levinas suggests that the very existence of the *I* is wrapped up in the existence of the *other*, so that I am responsible for the other's well-being. Indeed, my own well-being depends on it (xii–xiii; cf. Warren 2014, 186). Such thinking for Levinas leads him to suggest that the other is a fundamental ontology that is at once *not* an ontology (8–11). In a certain sense, the presence of others is a phenomenological (experiential) reality that insists on an ontological ethic of relational responsibility (8). To say so plainly, the foundation of ethics is to care for others because of the ontology of human relationships; a self becomes essential because of the presence of an other.

For Bonhoeffer, such a commitment to a life lived for the good of others resulted in activity that violated his own convictions and personal sense of righteousness. His participation in the failed *putsch* (coup) of July 20, 1943, against Adolf Hitler was not a denial of his pacifist convictions but was a violation of his personal righteousness on behalf of others (see Todt [2007, 117ff] for further discussion on this point). Such epistemic dissonance is an extreme example and is perhaps beyond the pale of what I am trying to say about ethics in music. It does, however, highlight several salient features of Christian ethics that have significance for my argument here: (1) Bonhoeffer's commitment to living for the good of others led him to confront the unjust powers that surrounded him in Nazi Germany; (2) his acts of civil disobedience were not motivated by a commitment to an abstract ideal or a natural law but rather by a commitment to the concrete right to human, bodily life; (3) he was oriented around the idea of the flourishing of the other as the foundation of ethical living in the freedom of costly grace.

Bonhoeffer's view was that the ultimate reality of God is found in the penultimate reality of human beings by virtue of the incarnation—the God-human Jesus; I contend that Levinas's insistence on the idea of human identity and existence being bound up in the acknowledged presence of others (or an Other) provides a more comprehensive ontology of relationship by which we may frame an ethic of caring toward restorative justice.

Applying this point about the centrality of relationships to Warren's argument for musical responsibility suggests that our responsibility to others through musical activity is to care for them by responding to their needs and to accept in reciprocal kind the care they offer to us. As I have argued throughout this book, musical activity participates in these acts of loving justly by virtue of its discursive/meaningful and formative/affective power; musicking can at once care for the other and care for the self. Yet such an application implicitly reveals how the constraints on human agency are often encountered in systems of power, as Kevin's reflections on police brutality and "President Trump" suggest. Indeed, there is a profound danger in reading Gustafson's suggestion that "God" "is or is in" the power structures that bear down on us as unreservedly sanctioning the actions of those power structures and their occupants.

Navigating Power and Relational Ethics in and through Music

The fact that there are power positions is a messy and difficult reality of life. Because of these differentials, the word "power" itself often carries connotations of abuse and oppression. This is not necessarily the case in every circumstance for, as Theodore Kemper contends, positions of power are an inherent part of human life; they are not inherently oppressive or liberating, but can be either—or both (2011).

The reality of power is an important aspect to consider in musical ethics—especially in the context of Christian communities. Who is in a position of power? Or who has greater agency in a given situation? To return to the example of Bonhoeffer, who was the power he was addressing? While the obvious answer is Nazism, it is important to note that Bonhoeffer himself occupied a position of ecclesial and social power that enabled him to advocate for the right to life and flourishing of those with less power—those persecuted by an unjust regime, who eventually included himself.

In this way, we can see how the life of care for the other can and should lead to a confrontation with unjust power. How would such a confrontation look in congregational music as considered in this book? It would be instructive to examine such music in relation to a specific example of justice work, for example, the conversation between Samantha, Ron, and Nick from Chapter 1 regarding using hip-hop music for worship in Samantha's "old, white" Anglican church. Samantha affirmed that she was responsible to her congregants musically, and that part of that responsibility was to protect their relational needs and to facilitate their worship by not offending their sensibilities. This draws the question out into the open. In so doing, it projects ethical music discourse (that is, the meanings, values, and convictions attached to/mediated by certain genres of music) into the mix of care and justice while theoretically highlighting the tension inherent in that relationship of care to justice. This care/justice tension is further revealed when considered through the lens of power relations. The congregation of Samantha's church would likely be irritated by her use of hip-hop music during the service, and this musical selection would perhaps damage the relationship she has cultivated with the congregation. Yet a commitment to justice may well compel her to violate that relationship: if Samantha became convinced that her congregation was participating in an unjust system of power structures that privilege white people over black people, then she may indeed have an ethical responsibility to her congregation to perform rap music during worship. As several scholars have argued, rap and hip-hop music are explicit confrontations of unjust racial power in America (Boyd 2003, 2007; Gammage 2017; Brooks and Martin 2019; Ford 2019, for instance), and perhaps would, within a certain discursive perspective and with acute sensitivity to context, be an appropriate way of mediating a challenge and rebuke to a congregation.

On the one hand, a certain version of care ethics alone would argue that such an intervention would be unethical because it would violate the ontology of relationships in which intimacy is primary: Samantha would surely rupture some relationships in her congregation by such an action. How might the relational ethics I am arguing for facilitate such an intervention, depending on certain other contextual factors?

Assuming the need for relationships to be just in order to be healthy could be understood to impel a disruption of certain power structures in order to facilitate relational health through justice. Pursuing this hypothetical example yields some insight. Suppose the congregation started being confronted with its racism; perhaps several black families began attending, and the white congregants resented that fact. Perhaps some were passively (or actively) trying to make the new families leave—or perhaps make sure they knew that they were the second-class congregants. If that were the case, Samantha would have an ethical responsibility to intervene musically. Such a determination would of course depend on the principle of attentiveness that underpins care ethics, and it would, from the perspective of restorative caring, need to be done in a manner that maximizes the chances of people being restored to relationships with others.

Alternatively, suppose that the realization of unjust racial systems occurred within the generational relations of the white congregation; perhaps the children or grandchildren of the older congregants began to realize that their elders were engaged in such racist power structures and sought to correct their relatives. Now suppose that attempt at correction resulted in a falling out between the family members; maybe they would not even sit on the same sides of the sanctuary with each other. In such a scenario, would performing hip-hop music in worship be a just and caring intervention if Samantha were able to leverage her relationships with the elder congregants to facilitate restoration with their loved ones?

In still another imagined scenario, suppose that through some archival work in the financial records it became immediately evident that the church's financial systems were intimately implicated in the North American project of whiteness. Maybe the seed money that founded the congregation was generated by exploiting slave labor, or perhaps the church's endowment was structured to profit from real estate laws designed to keep people of color out of the most desirable neighborhoods. Would the redress afforded by hip-hop's blatant affront to the commercial interests of whiteness serve to turn the congregation toward anti-racism, or would it cause them to double-down on their financial interests (Lipsitz 2018)?

In either case, it is difficult to imagine that using hip-hop in worship in Samantha's congregation would be effective in any capacity for restoring congregants to just relationships with each other or in actively moving toward social anti-racism. Instead, perhaps Samantha would borrow an approach that many other congregations have chosen in reflexively addressing issues of racial oppression and power structures. During my fieldwork at Lakeshore, I observed on several occasions that the music minister would include a non-Western Christian musical selection from what is commonly referred to as the "global song" repertory (Moore 2017). In one instance, the mostly middle-aged choir attempted to lead the congregation in a "Traditional Cameroonian" dance that accompanied the song "Stand, oh, Stand Firm."[8] Most of the predominantly white congregants gamely attempted to sing, clap, and move their bodies at the same time (to varying degrees of success), but I noticed a few exasperated expressions and embarrassed grimaces on the part of several congregants. It was several months before Lakeshore attempted another global song in worship.

As Marissa Glynias Moore points out, many practitioners of global song are members of white, liberal protestant churches who recognize the injustices of colonialism and missionization efforts from the previous centuries and seek to participate in the global church by "singing the world" (11). C. Michael Hawn calls this "praying with" others by using their prayers (2003, 13) and argues that this practice can be interpreted as a countercultural opposition to Western musical hegemony (7–15).

Yet as Moore points out, there are myriad problems that churches face when attempting to sing this repertoire. The most prominent of these is that it is nearly impossible to practice global song with full assurance of authentic translation/performance, which is imperative for guarding against appropriation and letting other cultures "lead," so to speak, and thus placing the white, Western congregations into a position of humility (Moore 2017, 13–14). Moreover, she notes that it is difficult to account for the often unrecognized ubiquity of Euro-American cultural power, and attempts at parity that fail to reckon with this ubiquity often further institutionalized oppressive cultural power (14; see also Lipsitz 2018).

Additionally, within the discourse of global song, there is an aspect of what Timothy Rommen calls "the negotiation of proximity" (2007, 57). Speaking of Full Gospel Churches in Trinidad singing North American Gospel tunes instead of gospelypso for worship, Rommen notes that it is far easier to sing the song of a distant other than a proximate other, as less is known of the distant other and thus their "difference" is less troubling to a dominant group (56–60). For global song practitioners, a hymn or sacred song from Brazil or Cameroon (that may have musical elements associated with pagan or at least secular practices there) has fewer cultural connotations than Christian hip-hop or Christian punk rock and is therefore easier to incorporate in musical worship than styles about which more is known to be troubling.

Attempts to "pray with others" in global song such as Lakeshore's are often awkward, as the congregation is rarely familiar with the musical forms or adept at their performance. However, as Moore suggests, "while global song practice is far from perfect, it represents an attempt to embody both cultural particularities and the widespread spiritual communion of the global church" (2017, 15) in a manner that attempts to justly acknowledge the differences of others. Moore's work suggests that global song can be used successfully to address these unjust cultural power differentials in certain congregations but that such successes are challenging and difficult to attain; and as I have suggested elsewhere, persons who occupy privileged positions of power would do well to cease attempting to lead such efforts (Myrick 2018c).

As should be clear by now, I am arguing that treating musical genre in such a morally discursive manner is ineffective at best and destructive at worst. It is true that for many, generic understandings are how they experience other people during musical activity, but such understandings are limited by myriad factors: location, time, cultural competency, cultural origin, and so on. Recall CJ's and Bob's reflections on Lakeshore's musical style in concert with Lakeshore's congregants' self-understanding of its music from Chapter 1: CJ, being from California, interpreted Lakeshore's music as being stuffy, out of touch, and antithetical to his values of inclusion and progress; Bob's account of his friend who struggled with the triggering effect of Lakeshore's music due to associations with Southern Baptist congregations conveyed similar implications. Yet Lakeshore's leadership and many of its members understood their music as subversive and resistant to the regressive, "fundamentalist" factions in Baptist polity who had "taken over" the SBC. This demonstrates that musical genres are unreliable means of discursively pursuing ethics and goodness.

Consistent engagement with a certain musical expression such as a genre may indeed form associations between the genre and certain values and convictions—and therefore become meaningful; however, such formation does not necessarily ensure goodness or flourishing. Moreover, the instability of meaning and consequent divergent modes of formation make using genre as an ethical antidote to injustice ineffectual in communities. Furthermore, it becomes clear that such use does damage to individuals due to the vulnerable criteria of authenticity; if an individual were to expose a preference for contemporary worship music in a congregation that associated that genre with immorality or regressive politics, that individual's place in the community could be jeopardized. If this is so, then it follows that using a different genre of music to confront members with injustice, such as hip-hop in the hypothetical example of Samantha's congregation, would be similarly ineffective or even deleterious.

Instead, keeping the ontology of relationships in view reveals that attentiveness and reciprocity provide helpful frames for just and caring responses to such scenarios. Attentiveness to the relationships within the congregation can inform a leader's actions in appropriate ways; reciprocity demands that if a different genre is used, it is used in a manner that does not violate the integrity of those whose vulnerable identities are bound up in its performance.

Yet there is more to say about the intersection of power and racial privilege in North America. Kevin's example of the prayer service at the beginning of this chapter provides a helpful example of how a congregation may respond to unjust power and social injustice in a caring manner. Yet as Kevin noted, his congregants' experience of injustice was largely one of observation: they *saw* it happening to others, and that grieved them, but it was not generally immanent to their everyday lives. For others, the threat of violence and injustice is ever-present and very immanent. How can music in Christian communities respond to immediate, bodily injustice in caring ways? An event I observed during worship at Greater Ebenezer gives a concrete example of how musical activity itself can indeed respond in real time.

A Hospitable Defense: Observation from Greater Ebenezer Baptist Church

February 4, 2018. *During the children's sermon at Greater Ebenezer Baptist Church, a young white man enters the sanctuary when the ushers open the doors after prayer. He has a peculiar look about him, dressed in athletic shorts, combat boots, an oversized sweater, and a soccer club scarf draped across his shoulders (I could not see which club). A large, styrofoam "Whataburger" cup is in his hand. There is a nervous energy about him that makes me anxious. He wanders to the front of the sanctuary where a deacon meets him and offers him a seat in the second row. The man takes the seat and looks around the room while the children's sermon is being delivered.*

Ebenezer has a weekly tradition of acknowledging their visitors following the Children's Sermon, asking them to stand and introduce themselves. The young man stands and introduces himself as Malchizadek, the high priest of Jehovah Most High. "I have come to deliver a message should I find hospitable fellowship here." A voice from the congregation testifies, "Go ahead," and Malchizadek continues to deliver a minute-long utterance that vacillates between warning and congratulating, revealing a deeply disturbed mind. The worship leader welcomes Malchizadek, but a sense of unease settles over the room. Having introduced myself, I watch Malchizadek as the worship leader announces tithes and offering. Reggie, the drummer and saxophonist, strikes a driving tempo for "Fire Shut Up in My Bones." Robert, the piano player, joins him in a pulsing rendition of the tune. The choir struggles a bit at first, like the song was unplanned. Reggie takes the lead and sings the chorus. Soon, the choir has it and so does the congregation. The ushers have not moved, despite the announcement of tithes and offerings. As we are singing, I notice Malchizadek get up and walk over to where one of the offering baskets is resting on the end of a pew, take what appear to be Easter eggs out of his Whataburger cup, and place them into the basket. He then walks toward the back of the sanctuary using the side aisle, along the wall immediately to my right. Sitting in the second to last row, I have a clear view of his movements until he passes me. As he does so, I sense him stop. I glance quickly over my right shoulder and notice him standing immediately behind me, alone in the last row of pews (as I am in mine). I turn back to the front of the sanctuary, unsure of what will happen next. After a brief moment, I sense Malchizadek leaving. I turn and watch him walk out the door. A moment or two after he leaves, the deacon who had ushered him to a seat retrieves the "eggs" (someone later told me they were lemons) from the basket and places them on the floor next to the pews. He then takes the basket and the congregation is invited to stand and bring their offerings to the altar, where the deacons have now brought the baskets along with the two-foot by eighteen-inch wooden model of a church with a slot on top through which to drop money. Reggie, Robert, and the choir continuing playing "Fire" as the congregation places their offerings in the baskets and symbolically in the "church."

Music for Others

Two weeks after Malchizadek's visit to Greater Ebenezer, over breakfast at IHOP, I asked Reggie if he remembered the affair and what he made of it. He remembered and shared my sentiments of concern over Malchizadek's words and actions: "I was like, 'So, did you come in to end my life or did you come in to say this prayer for me on the street?' " When I asked him about his choice of "Fire," he confessed that he does not even remember what song he played: "I wish I knew!" Moreover, he does not remember any of the details about the congregation's response, likely, he said, because he was watching closely to see what Malchizadek would do next.

Though Reggie did not recall the song he chose in the heat of the moment, his choice was profound and significant. Analyzing the choice of song in the tense situation described reveals one way that musical activity can justly respond in caring, affective ways to a potentially dangerous situation. I can make no claim as to what Malchezadek's intentions were, but it appeared as though there was something about the music that either satisfied or repelled him. It also seems like more than coincidence that the lyrics of the song Reggie chose in the heat of the moment describe the words of a prophet. It could have been that Reggie was reaching out in a musical way to the service's unusual guest, giving him a prophetic text with which to identify and, in doing so, giving the members of the congregation a sympathetic frame through which they could interpret their guest's strange actions. In this way, the musical response could be interpreted as hospitable, even welcoming, to the volatile and potentially dangerous stranger.

> It's just like fire, shut up in my bones.
> It's the Holy Ghost fire, shut up in my bones.
> It's just like fire, and it's shut up in my bones.
> It's the Holy Ghost fire, and it's shut up in my bones.
>
> From his mother's belly, Born to prophesy.
> The prophet Jeremiah, Would lift his voice and cry.
> Be quiet folks commanded, Shut up leave us alone.
> How can you be quiet, When there's fire down in your bones.

The song's lyrical theme of fire was paralleled in its driving beat and quick tempo; it seemed to represent a Holy Ghost fire that could not be contained. On the other hand, the driving beat and quick tempo were a stark departure from the other songs we had sung that morning and could be understood as both hospitable and as responsorial; it very much matches the tone of the lyrics, and conveys a sense of almost defiant confidence in a prophetic calling. What I observed was that the performance of "Fire" that morning embodied both hospitality and defense at the same time. In this instance the musical activity itself was a response that was both hospitable and caring, but it was also acting on behalf of the well-being of the congregation, both as encouragement and as comfort. Perhaps as a result of this highly appropriate—and I would contend, profoundly ethical—musical response, Malchizadek left without doing any harm, alleviating fears and bolstering the praise of the congregation.[9]

Think again of the hypothetical example of Samantha's congregation. The issue with musical genre or style in worship was not one of aesthetics per se but rather was one of race. While planning selections from the global song repertory may afford an opportunity for the congregation to "pray with others" from around the world, such an act alone would never have been able to reckon with the reality of systemic racial injustice in the United States. The hypothetical problem in this hypothetical scenario is not whether white congregations should perform music that ostensibly "belongs" to another culture; rather, the problem is that white churches are unwilling to acknowledge that their way of being in the world is neither advocating the advancement of their black brothers and sisters nor aware that such advancement is needed.

If Samantha were to become convinced that her "old, white" Anglican church needed to become more actively involved in racial restitution through reconciliation and reparation, her best course of action would be to ask if she and her choir or music team could visit a black church from her denomination and learn from them. Attend the services. Learn the songs, the patterns, the techniques. Learn to *listen*. Not as *allies*, who, in their freedom are working to free the oppressed, but as those who are working for *their own freedom* from oppression in an unjust system, those who realize that their freedom is bound up together in the freedom and equality of their black family.

For those who would become allies and advocates, black communities such as Greater Ebenezer have developed profound, effective techniques for thriving in a society that is hostile to their very presence—to say nothing of their flourishing. Let them take the lead and support them as and when you are able. Embrace the reality of being in relationship with those communities (your flourishing is bound up in theirs), and then *be for* them. Instead of making their music "work for you," let your music be for others.

Conclusion

The Relational Ethics of Music for Others

> If one is to acknowledge another as one's neighbor, one must acknowledge oneself as his or her neighbor.
>
> —Stanley Cavell (The Claim of Reason, 434)

The Relationship of Authenticity to Aesthetics

As I have written and re-written the words that have appeared in these pages, I have pondered again how authenticity and personal honesty leverage themselves into relational matrices. When I say that relationships are ontological for both humans and music, I mean that they are not aspirational, as in, relationships are not the *telos* of human existence. Instead, I mean that they are the *foundation* of existence. The *telos,* such as there is one, is for *good*, that is, *healthy* relationships: *good realities.* Justice—by definition—is the necessary condition of good reality. I make these statements broadly. And indeed, they seem to add up. But when I bring these pseudo-syllogisms out of the ether and start thinking through their efficacy in real life, it becomes immediately clear that there is far more complexity and many more intersecting streams of value and impulse in musical activities. Doubly so for music in Christian communities. While I have tried to bring out the nuances and particularities of this complexity through ethnographic fieldwork in this book, I believe that I have not yet satisfactorily answered the question of authenticity in congregational music.

I have been struck by how often authenticity is noted as the definitive criterion of "good" music. For many, authenticity means being vulnerable in Christian communities, being honest to your fellows about your loves, values, and convictions. It is no accident that this criterion of good music is also a central criterion of good relationships—*good realities*.

Music for Others. Nathan Myrick, Oxford University Press (2021). © Oxford University Press.
DOI: 10.1093/oso/9780197550625.003.0006

It is precisely at this point that aesthetics and ethics collide. While I have hardly said a word about aesthetics in this book (and that is on purpose), here in the conclusion I must add a few words. If what makes music good is honesty and vulnerability, bringing the depth of being to bear on an experience, then here we have encountered space for considering ethics in music without trying to subject music to the demands of empowered morality. Yet this acknowledgment does not necessarily resolve the issues that have plagued meditations on aesthetics and ethics for centuries. Instead, care ethics, as I have argued in the preceding chapters, provides a way of embracing this intersection and considering the particularities and commitments of each.

What does authenticity look like when viewed through the lens of care oriented toward restorative justice? It looks like making space for others to be honest—without controlling the orientation of that honesty. It looks like paying attention to others—without doing so for the sake of gaining leverage for coercion. It looks like acknowledging your own position as an other to them—recognizing your own neighborliness. This acknowledgment is profoundly vulnerable. Humility in the form of disowning the privileges or power we occupy in order to place ourselves in the community as a peer cuts both ways across the grain of ego and prejudice. A community that practices care through restorative justice must be willing to celebrate the diversity and real differences that real people bring to that community with personal and cultural humility. A caring community will always be open to embracing the diversity of humanity, working tirelessly to ensure the full flourishing of each.

This diversity does not necessarily always mean musical form, style, or genre. Instead, it means withholding judgment from a leader or congregant who might disagree about what constitutes "orthodoxy." It means actively working to preserve the space for others and selves to honestly express both needs and capabilities so as to enable flourishing for all. It means being aware of how my own agency limits the agency of the other, yet is necessary for good realities. It means refusing to conflate entire identities with musical genres or gesture—perhaps in the "cosmopolitan" manner that Porter suggests. It means keeping the human impulse to control others in check.

From this description of what a posture of care might look like in Christian communities, the questions that scholars of sacred music often address are reconsidered. Care means holding open spaces for the tastes of others to be celebrated. It also means orienting our own tastes toward good realities, that is, just relationships. If our aesthetic preferences achieve ontological status, then we must assume they have violated the primacy of relationship and are therefore being applied unjustly. For this reason, I am deeply suspicious of scholars who consider "beauty" to be an objective category. Not that beauty is unimportant. It is deeply important. But it is not a moral category of the senses. The most aesthetically ugly things are sometimes the most morally beautiful—if we are paying attention.

Lyrics, Actions, and Human Flourishing

Despite my efforts to address the aspects of music that have been under-addressed by other sacred music scholars, this account of ethics in musical activity would be incomplete without acknowledging the role that lyrics play in both the construction of meaning and the didactic content that congregational music can mediate. Many of my conversation partners indeed spoke of the lyrical content as very important, both in terms of what music means and how it makes them feel. As Lakeshore's associate pastor Sharlande Sledge said, "The words are very important." This was affirmed by each church leader I spoke to and also by several congregants. For example, Kory, a recent seminary graduate who managed a coffee shop in Waco at the time of our interview, responded to my question of responsibility by saying the texts of Lakeshore's music inspired him to care for the needs of the oppressed around him as an act of justice:

> The assumption that I have is that it's an accountability towards what we're singing, but also to the greater picture of "do justice, love mercy and walk humbly with God." To "take care of the orphans and the widows and seek out and protect the oppressed."

As a person who had been trained to occupy a position of leadership in a given community, he described this accountability in terms of community building and relationships within the church, noting "The Servant's Song," a benedictional hymn for Lakeshore, as being particularly important in this regard:

> [The lyrics] "walk the mile, bear the load" [are very important], I think that this is a shared commitment within a community and my singing this with each and every other person is me asking them to keep me

> accountable, and also me telling them that I'm gonna keep them accountable, and asking for each other, for us both to join each other in this shared commitment.

As Kory's reflection indicates, the lyrics are very important in musical worship, as they serve to provide an easy point of reference for determining the meaning of the piece and its ethical merit. As I have argued in the preceding chapters, the lyrics of musical worship are only one component of its efficacy and impact, yet their evaluation is an important aspect of congregational music's ethical significance.

Conclusion: Care, Justice, and Relationships

Throughout this book, I have argued that music's way of being in the world is inherently relational and that this dynamic relational ontology encompasses both meaning and emotion; that in musical activity meaning and affect, reason and emotion, converge in human bodies. This dyadic convergence can (and often does) configure and orient our understanding of self and others together with the ways our social imaginaries occupy the gaps between self and other that are uncovered by such understanding. With this in mind, it is clear that music is ethically significant, and I have further argued that this significance can be understood as care wedded to restorative justice. From the perspective of the discourse ethics favored by musicologists and ethnomusicologists, I noted that music can indeed be understood as ethical discourse through genre and style (in addition to the lyrics, of which an ocean of ink has been put to page by others), but that such a frame does not account for the fact that these conventions of meaning-making are often quite unethically oriented against each other. Further still, when considered from an ecclesiological perspective, the antagonistic meanings of genre as revealed in the "worship wars" indicates that examining music in Christian communities from the perspective of discourse ethics is not in itself a sufficient ethical theory for those who comprise that community, but instead it demonstrates the need for one.

Likewise, from the perspective of character formation ethics favored by liturgical theologians and church music scholars, I demonstrated that musical activity does indeed form identities and communities by virtue of its ability to marshal human emotions and affections and that doing so often influences understandings of selves and others through how we feel about them or our relationship with them. But formation also is not a sufficient ethical theory, because however helpful it may be, in its best iterations it reveals only how ethical character is formed but does not afford a means of evaluating or planning toward that formation. How can congregational music form individual character in ethical ways if the absolute meaning of music and lyrics is unreliable, as I argued in Chapter 1? Indeed, as is particularly prevalent in confessional scholarship on music in Christian worship, a complete trust in the absolute efficacy of orthodoxy for ethical formation leads to an application of formation ethics to musical activity that affords and even demands violation of relational justice.

Music is relationally ordered sound, and as Warren and others point out, every musical experience involves an encounter with another human, either directly or indirectly. This relational way of being in the world rests on two interwoven strands of meaning and affection. Meaning is made by the convergence and subsequent configuring of expressions and gestures that correspond to sonic and social values and convictions determined discursively in community. Musical meaning is negotiated stylistically and performatively, with certain values or convictions being affirmed or rejected according to the conventions of the genre. Such discursive activity in music parallels language in a limited sense; genres can be thought of as languages within which certain sounds and gestures are capable of meaning something. Yet as Feld and Fox point out, the semantic indefiniteness of music makes musical meaning even more unstable than that of language, and musical meaning is often therefore determined by linguistic exchange—by talking about what music means. In this way, musical meaning is determined in the context of community. This way of meaning-making also works in reverse, as communities form around shared understanding of musical meaning even as they continue to negotiate that shared understanding.

However, musical meaning is always determined in relation to musical feeling; how a piece or genre of music makes us feel is integral to what it means. The second interwoven strand of music's ontology is how it invokes, engenders, or invites emotion in human beings. From the perspective of contour theory, music invokes emotion by way of imitation; musical activity also influences human emotion through entrainment, the phenomenon of human bodily rhythms synchronizing such that emotion is elicited. This invocation of emotion has profound efficacy when experienced with other people, and an important aspect of music's relational ontology is the way that our emotional responses to musical activity are associated with others. Indeed, this association suggests that musical activity plays a profound and particular role in constructing "social imaginaries," the way we perceive and believe our relationships with others to be. Social imaginaries are further configured in musical activity by the activity's "feelingfulness," that is, the way that musical experiences affectively index memories of relationships with others. To paraphrase, singing with others may help us negotiate how we feel about our relationships with others; when we are angry with someone, singing with them helps to manage our anger and imagine our relationships more charitably. This connection of emotion to relationships reveals how musical activity influences human affections, our loves and desires, and how the convergence of meaning and emotion in human bodies configures affection toward people, objects, and ideals.

This account of music's relational ontology suggests that (1) music is ethically significant and that (2) an ethical theory of music must be able to give a comprehensive account of human relationships. Musical discourse ethics, such as the ethics of style (Rommen 2007) and cosmopolitan musical ethics (Porter 2016), afford fruitful ways of thinking about how musical genres and styles have moral importance. Indeed, each person I interviewed understood musical style as a fundamental way that music communicates and makes meaning and therefore is ethically significant, affirming the basic tenet of musical discourse ethics that through shared understandings of musical meaning, values and convictions are negotiated and individual and communal identities are configured.

However, what genres and styles *mean* is profoundly unstable, varying from group to group and place to place to so great a degree that the lack of agreement over musical meaning renders the negotiation of values and convictions through musical genre insufficient. Using the example of the "worship wars," I showed that negotiation of values and convictions through musical genre and style breaks down due to disagreements over musical meaning, resulting in musical communities and congregations that are mutually opposed to one another by definition and thereby undercutting the principles of ethical discourse. For Christian communities, such mutual opposition is incompatible with the ecclesial vision confessed by many of these communities for the unity of all Christians in faith. But more than that, considering musical ethics from the perspective of discourse reveals that conflicts over style in musical worship are in actuality the result of our need to know and control others; music confronts us with ourselves, with our loves and desires, but we also encounter others in musical activity in ways that we cannot control.

The relational ethics of music provides a means of evaluating how music is employed as normative, ritual activity in Christian communities. This requires recognizing that through music, congregation members and leaders are given the unique ability to care for the emotions and affections of a congregation while also orienting the congregation members' understanding of self and other in ways that are often difficult to identify in real time. Thinking with Held (2006) and Nussbaum (2002, 2011), congregational music is caring, then, when it is practiced and performed with attention to the needs and desires of the congregation; when the humanity and agency of those who exhibit those needs and desires is acknowledged and respected; when they are acknowledged respectfully and responded to equitably as each person is able: response-ability (Cobussen and Nielsen 2012; Warren 2014).

Second, music is caring when it orients the emotional posture of the community toward restorative justice-as-human-flourishing. Sometimes, this may mean speaking truth to uncaring power, in the local community and to the world writ large. It also involves affording space for the voices of the community to be heard by others—especially those who may not hear such a voice except in the sanctuary. Perhaps, as Kevin suggested, this may be accomplished in a prayer service that incorporates music through which the congregation can sing their prayers, giving affective voice to their needs and desires, hopes and fears, in the hospitable presence of others afforded by the music. Or, as my experiences at Greater Ebenezer suggest, it may be a response to a potential threat that neither escalates nor ignores the situation but rather defuses the threat through hospitably, shifting the orientation of the congregation toward a solution. Perhaps that piece of music can act as a symbolic refrain that invokes the congregation's response-ability to each other and to the world each time it is performed, as "The Servant's Song" does at Lakeshore. In a like manner, music can also subvert the voices of uncaring power much as Floyd (1996) and Southern (1979 [1983]) suggest in their work on spirituals, blues, and gospel music. Such an endeavor must be done with great attentiveness and concern for the well-being of the congregation while acknowledging that it might result in further relational rupture, as my reading of Bonhoeffer suggests for the hypothetical scenario of Samantha's "old, white, Anglican church."

Finally, music is ethical when it heals; when it restores minds, bodies, and emotions to relational health; when it repairs broken and fractious relationships through its embodiment of the other, or through its symbolic representation of mutual values, or through its affective convictions of injustice.[1] Healing also includes invoking concern for justice in the community and between churches and the worlds they inhabit. Music reminds us that if the church promotes injustice, it cannot be an agent in the healing of the world; further, it calls us to imaginative responses to the claims of restorative justice. In this, church music can heal by helping congregations imagine better worlds and by orienting the affections of the congregation toward generating those kinds of worlds that are centered on calling human beings to just and therefore healthy relationships with each other and by extension with God.

Suggestions for Further Research

Much work remains to be done in this area. While I have built on the work of many scholars, the relative dearth of research on ethics of and within music in Christian communities remains. I hope that, while this book is by no means the first word on the matter, it will also not be the last.

Although I have focused my efforts on music in Christian communities, I have drawn from conversations in ethics, theology, and several branches of music scholarship, and in so doing I have attempted to frame my constructions in ways that will also speak back to the conversations from which I draw. Such attempts inevitably require more work than a single volume can manage, and further research will certainly make these exchanges more effective. For instance, this book has only mildly engaged virtue ethics, and even then only in its more explicitly ecclesial forms; a more robust account of virtue theory will enhance both my affirmation of formation and my critique of its efficacy for ethical evaluation. Additionally, I have not engaged a rigorous examination of belief structures and systems that likely play an important role in understanding how individuals and communities form and express values and convictions. Engaging epistemologies of belief will likely enhance our understanding of individual and communal values and convictions, and therefore relational ethics.

This book has not examined several other aspects of music's way of being in the world that can and likely do pertain to Christian communities more broadly. For instance, I have only briefly engaged conversations on the effects of aesthetics on musical worship and their link to ethics. Additionally, I have only made passing mention of the role of entertainment in contributing positively as well as negatively to human flourishing. What significance might entertainment, on the one hand, or a sense of the sublime, on the other, have in the relational ethics of music in Christian communities? *Should* music in worship be entertaining? Is greater responsibility invoked by "beautiful" music?

Final Thoughts

One thing is clear: human relationships matter. By and large, many have undervalued the relational ethics of musical activity. By directing our focus toward meaning, expression, identity, and rights—and especially taste, style, structure, and the lyrics in light of theological orthodoxy on the part of confessional scholars—we have undermined our own efforts to enable and encourage honest and healthy musical practices because we have done so at the expense of the relationships that music depends on. Too often, conversations about musical worship focus on the didactic aspects of that activity at the expense of the relational, "reduc[ing] music to a commodified object" (Warren 2014, 1). My hope for this book is to work against that trend.

For scholars, relational ethics encourages us to acknowledge and embrace the instability of musical meaning together with its uncontrollable affective elements and frame our prescriptions in light of these realities. For practitioners, ethical congregational music leadership involves actively listening to both the individual congregants' and the congregation's needs and seeking to respond to them in real time *without* seeking to control their responses, values, and convictions. Caring musical practice makes space for the prayers of others and gives voice to the loves and desires of people. Perhaps this is a prayer service such as that suggested by Kevin, where the congregants were able to sing their prayers over a short vamp and have them echoed by the others. Perhaps it is hospitality that affirms even the most seemingly obtuse person in the congregation—or protects the congregation from threat—or perhaps it would involve introducing bodily actions like turning to face each other for the benediction. In any situation, it will necessarily require attentiveness to the needs and diversity of a congregation and a willingness to serve others musically. For all of us, the relational ethics of music reminds us again and again of our neighbors, calling us to acknowledge and celebrate their full humanity, their agency and their difference, acting in music and beyond in order to facilitate their love of others in the context of human flourishing.

Notes

Introduction

1. These are pseudonyms. In order to maintain privacy, none of my interlocutors' real names are used, excepting when they are a public figure (such as a pastor of a church) whose identity cannot effectively be hidden.
2. I draw this term from phenomenologists such as Martin Heidegger and others, although I first encountered it in Dietrich Bonhoeffer's *Ethics* (1949 [2005]). By it I mean the "activity of existing"; the phenomenological existence of something as it is encountered by other somethings in time and space; its dynamic and discrete ontology. In saying this, I do not mean that music is a self-sustaining entity or moral agent, but rather that it occurs in real life and has effects that are experienced, interpreted, and remembered bodily, such that music is also always a relational something. See Heidegger (1996); cf. Phillips (2015) and Wheeler (2017).
3. I am using this term to invoke the discourse ethics of Jürgen Habermas. If one refuses (tacitly or otherwise) to participate in the act of communal discussion and agreement of rights and goods, then discursive ethics are non-functioning. Timothy Rommen (2007) and Mark Porter (2016) elaborate on Habermas's ethics in their monographs engaged in Chapter 1. See Habermas (1990) for more on this.
4. The writings of Mark Porter (2016) and Jonathan Dueck (2017) present notable exceptions to this generalization, and their work will be engaged in the coming chapters.
5. J. Nathan Corbitt's *The Sound of the Harvest* (1998) is a prime example of this kind of scholarship whose intention is to provide a practical resource for congregational music practitioners, rather than to theorize about music and ethics. This is a great shame, as ethical theorization and reflection helps to prevent one from falling into myopic and self-sustaining claims about "good music."
6. James Frank Caccamo's dissertation (2004) is a notable exception to this trend and is considered further in Chapter 2.
7. It should be noted that from other perspectives music may be understood to have agentive qualities, perhaps even to have a kind of non-human agency. For example, Bernd Brabec de Mori argues for an understanding of music as an agent against Eurocentric understandings of both music and agency. Using Gell's (1998) definition of agency as any entity that breaks the chain of causality, Brabec de Mori points out that many musicians from both Eurocentric and non-Eurocentric traditions often attribute their inspiration to non-human agents, such as deities and muses. Furthermore, drawing on Levinson's (1990) "persona theory," de Mori observes that listeners often identify emotional personas as agents in the music and attribute something of their emotional responses to that agency (often attributed to the author or performer of the song by my conversation partners). See Brabec de Mori (2017).

8. The example of trying a misbehaving dog in medieval courts would be laughable save for its implications (see Taylor [2003] for more). This particular line of thought raises different ethical questions relating to ontology: Is a "good" dog one that does not bite, or is the "good" dog the one that does? Does it depend on what the purpose of a dog is and how well it fulfills that purpose (teleology)? To further illustrate this point, substitute the word "wolf" for "dog": What is a "good" wolf? Is it one that behaves as wolves ought, hunting and chasing and biting? Or is it one that abandons those activities and conforms to human standards of "goodness"? My point in this is that even when we may put a violent or ill animal down for its own good or the good of a community, we are not ascribing moral culpability to it on its own terms, but rather on ours, thus establishing ourselves as the moral agent in this sense.
9. This presents something of a challenge in analyzing my ethnographic interviews, as many of my interlocutors speak about music as if it is an agent, or an abstract principle. For instance, during my fieldwork at SXSW, a Fuller student said that music "makes meaning" in the context of a discussion about what music does.
10. Although we may and should certainly note that Wagner's anti-Semitism lent itself particularly well to this abuse.
11. However, music affords certain effects and uses; just as a chair affords sitting (Cavell 1997) or a doorknob affords turning (Gibson 1979), so music affords affective responses. Jeff R. Warren argues that more than affording responses, music limits and configures human responses to its activities (2021). There is not space in this book for an argument about whether or not these criteria hold for humans as agents as well.
12. *The Chalice* is not alone in this emphasis. Several other denominations revised several canonical classics for their hymnals in the 1980s and 1990s. See Westerfield-Tucker (2008) for more on this.
13. For more information on "Modern Worship," see Ingalls et al. 2013; Lim and Ruth 2017; Ingalls 2018. One unique feature of Harris Creek's Sunwest campus is the presence of an armed guard in the fellowship hall and patrolling the grounds during the services. While interesting and surely of impact on the worship service, an analysis of this phenomenon falls beyond the bounds of this book.

Chapter 1

1. I use "communication" here to connect more concretely to the idea of music as discourse. Anna Nekola's use of "mediation" (2015), as that which mediates between ideas and concepts and people, is perhaps a better term for describing music's mode of communication. However, because I am engaging musical "meaning" from the perspective of discourse ethics, I use communication to more clearly connect to that body of work.
2. Porter offers a compelling and contextualized suggestion of the ways that musical styles are negotiated in churches and the effect these negotiations have on the identities formed in those congregations.
3. Some clarification of the term "discourse" is needed here, as the moral character of Christian music—both of the congregational and devotional varieties—has often been thought to be determined by the lyrical content alone. This assumption, obvious

as it is, often fails to reckon with the relationship between the lyrics and the musical performance, on the one hand, and the relationship between the musician's actions and the lyrics and sound, on the other, and the relationship between the lyrics, score, presentation, and the agency of the congregation on still another (this is a multi-handed monster). Discourse, then, is not merely concerned with the lyrics but must be understood to encompass both the verbal and stylistic/generic activities of congregational song more broadly.

4. While I affirm Porter's use of cosmopolitanism as a theory in his chosen congregational context, my research suggests that not all churches and congregants share the cosmopolitan ethos he identifies. In Waco, Texas, for example, the residual of the "worship wars" remains like a thick coating of cedar pollen on the hearts and minds of many congregants. Indeed, musical style is very much a bone of contention for worshippers in this and other parts of the United States—including such cosmopolitan places as Los Angeles (Myrick 2015, see the discussion in "The Dingman Hypothesis" section). Yet my point is not to quibble with Porter's conclusions (I agree with him that "cosmopolitanism" as he describes it is a more ethical means of negotiating differences in identity, values, and convictions) but rather to interpret my own research through the lens he offers and see how that vantage point advances my inquiry.
5. I return to this topic and conversation in Chapter 4.
6. So Rommen suggests that members of the Full Gospel Community in Trinidad understand the ethics of style.
7. This is a pseudonym, not the deceased's real name.
8. I do not count "modern hymns," such as those written by Keith Getty and Stuart Townend, in this tally. If those and other similar songs were included, the number would be well over 200. In addition to relying on Lim and Ruth's definition of "contemporary worship songs" as a musical style that adapted the forms of pop, folk, and rock music for use during worship services, as well as using "updated English" rather than the somewhat archaic language of traditional hymns (2017, 8–11), I am also using the criteria of copyright ownership and original method of production to distinguish contemporary worship songs from traditional hymns: songs that are copyrighted by a record company and were originally distributed via recorded facsimile (CDs, MP3s, etc.) rather than as scores in a song book are considered contemporary worship here (Ingalls 2014).
9. Much more can be said about this development, including the rise of *Passion* conferences and other such extra-denominational events that helped to popularize the new worship music. For more, see Busman 2015a; Ingalls (2008, 2011, 2018), Justice (2012), and Mall (2020).
10. For further discussion on the use of technology as a marker of musical genre in churches, see Lim and Ruth (2017) and Ingalls (2018).
11. This research was conducted during the spring and summer of 2015 in Los Angeles, California. Data collected were analyzed using genre theory, along with qualitative and quantitative methods.
12. For example, Peters (1994), Hamilton (1999), and York (2003).
13. Jonathan Dueck (2017) has argued that for his Canadian Mennonite interlocutors, the worship wars were primarily about an "aesthetics of encounter," where embodied

relationships were negotiated in theologically and even ethically loaded ways through music (5–6). I will discuss his work in coming chapters, although his robust and rigorous description of aesthetics and that description's attendant argument will have to be engaged at greater length in future research.

Chapter 2

1. See Stout (2001) for how some virtue ethicists negotiate the problem of culture and context.
2. Cherry is but one of many church music scholars who build their arguments about musical worship from this set of assumptions.
3. This critique is affirmed by Nicholas Sagovsky's review of Wannenwetsch's book (Sagovsky 2005).
4. The relative shortness of Drew's tenure indicates that the church has recently re-established itself after some tumultuous years, which Drew described during the course of our conversation.
5. I will engage her work at greater length in Chapter 3.
6. The term "emotional intelligence" has been brought to popular attention by Daniel Coleman in his 2006 book, *Emotional Intelligence*, although that book has drawn intense criticism. See Murphy (2006).
7. His point about rituals and sacred objects seemed to have pigeon-holed Durkheim's "sacred object" into an explicitly confessional Christian understanding of religion (although this is almost certainly the result of an off-handed comment). Indeed, many popular music scholars such as Christopher Partridge would argue that a "Brad Paisley" concert can be as sacred as any Sunday worship gathering. See Partridge (2017).
8. It should be noted that people can become entrained merely to the music, but such entrainment does not result in the same meaningful experience as singing together with other people, nor does it construct meaningful bonds of relationship with others in the same manner.
9. I argued that "when this ritual practice is performed as entraining participation in congregational music-making, a further depth of emotional significance may be achieved by virtue of physiological unity. This depth is then indexed symbolically and re-performed into being each time the activity is meaningfully engaged in (depending in part on the negotiation of relational power dynamics), resulting in a cycle of deeper and stronger commitment to the ritual of congregational singing" (2017, 92).
10. I flag "embodied" not as a way of distinguishing this kind of emotion from another such kind, but rather to emphasize the point that musical emotions are always embodied.

Chapter 3

1. For some, the Western concept of consonance based in the triad is viewed as inherently oppressive rather than hospitable (for example, McClary 2002, 77, 143).

2. Cf. Tong (2014, 160–161).
3. Nussbaum defines these as "1. Being able to live to the end of a human life of normal length. 2. Being able to have good health, including reproductive health; adequately nourished and sheltered. 3. Being able to move freely from place to place; secure against violent assault, including sexual assault and domestic violence; opportunities for sexual satisfaction and for choice in matters of reproduction. 4. Being able to use the senses, to imagine, think, and reason—and to do these things in a 'truly human' way, a way informed and cultivated by an adequate education; being able to use imagination and thought in connection with experiencing and producing works and events of one's own choice, religious, literary, musical, and so forth. 5. Being able to have attachments to things and people outside ourselves; to love those who love and care for us; to grieve at their absence; in general to love, to grieve, to experience longing, gratitude, and justified anger; not having one's emotional development blighted by fear or anxiety. 6. Being able to form a conception of the good and to engage in critical reflection about the planning of one's life. 7. (A) being able to live with and towards others, to recognize and show concern for other human beings, to engage in various forms of social interaction; to be able to imagine the situation of another; (B) Having the social bases of self-respect and non-humiliation; being able to be treated as a dignified being whose worth is equal to that of others. 8. Being able to live with concern for and in relation to animals, plants, and the world of nature. 9. Being able to laugh to play, to enjoy recreational activities. 10. (A) *Political.* Being able to participate effectively in political choices that govern one's life; having the right of political participation, protections of free speech and association. (B) *Material.* Being able to hold property and having property rights on an equal basis with others; having the right to seek employment on an equal basis with others; having the freedom from unwarranted search and seizure. Being able to work as a human being, exercising practical reason and entering into meaningful relationships of mutual recognition with other workers" (33–34).
4. Acknowledgment of agency and mutual respect for others is a critical aspect of feminist ethics generally and care ethics specifically. This observation reveals that what has been called "the problem of difference" is not so much a problem in itself but is rather problematically understood and addressed. Instead of attempting to speak for all in the sense of universals or essences, many feminist scholars argue that differences of opinion, experience, perspective, and agenda should be named, acknowledged, respected—and even celebrated. These ideas were expressed and codified in a special issue of *Journal of Feminist Studies in Religion* (1992). See Eugene (1992); Hunt, Townes, and Umansky (1992); Isasi-Díaz (1992); Plaskow (1992); and Pui-lan (1992) for more on this.
5. Please do not take my metaphor further than I mean it: I am not suggesting that a harmonious relationship between the three pitches based on Western art music theory is the proper way of conceiving a chord. I hope it is obvious that after the preceding account I mean it as no more than a heuristic device and not as a model for properly relating the three.
6. For example, Zehr (1990); Braithwaite (2002); Boyes-Watson, Krumholz, and Rich-Shea (2013).
7. For example, reciprocity, equality, mutually fulfilling, and so on; see Cahill (1996) and Cannon (2006).

Chapter 4

1. Philando Castille was a black man who was killed by a Saint Anthony police officer in the City of Falcon Heights, MN during a traffic stop on July 6, 2016 while seated in his car with his partner and four-year-old child seated with him. His death triggered mass outrage and an eventual charge of manslaughter against the officer, who was subsequently acquitted of all charges, sparking further outrage and the termination of his employment by the City of Saint Anthony.
2. Levinas defines morality as the individual rules of a single person or society, and he defines ethics as the principles that those rules are derived from. As such, morality is the diverse set of ways that ethical abstractions are made concrete in lived reality.
3. See also Ingalls (2018), chapter 1, for further discussion on the individualization of musical worship.
4. Fourteen said "no" in general and "yes" in church; 6 said "yes" to both; 5 said "no" to both; 3 said "yes" in general and "no" in church; all others were non-committal in their answers.
5. Hauerwas commends Aristotle's *Nicomachean Ethics*, which invokes the necessity of self-knowledge and love as a prerequisite for love of others, although Hauerwas mollifies the effect of this by insisting that such ability is dependent on God's revelation.
6. This inversion of the "golden rule" is more clearly evident in Luke's account of the same material (Luke 10:25–37). Instead of placing the words of the greatest commandment in Jesus's mouth, the author puts them into the mouth of the lawyer. When Jesus affirms the lawyer's exegesis, the lawyer wishes to justify himself and utters those words that have troubled Christians throughout history, "And who is my neighbor?" (29). Jesus responds with the parable of the Good Samaritan, where the logic is that you are also a neighbor. Your neighborliness is directed to whomever you encounter, but you have also received the care that a neighbor gives.
7. Action becomes profane when it is not oriented toward the flourishing of the other and therefore to the love of God.
8. #445 in *Lift Up Your Hearts: Psalms, Hymns, and Spiritual Songs* (2013).
9. In writing this book, I have often thought about what significance geo-spatial location—and racialized spaces in particular—have to do with acts of ecclesial violence, and in turn how mediatized narratives are constructed in response to those acts. Had Malchizadek arrived at Sunwest on a Sunday morning, with its armed guard patrolling the building, and had attempted to offer his prophetic utterance, the outcome might have been much different—and more tragic. As I mentioned in note 13 from the Introduction, this topic falls well beyond the scope of this book, but I cannot shake the feeling that there is something worth lingering on here. The incident at Greater Ebenezer occurred shortly after a gunman entered a small Baptist church in Sutherland Springs, Texas, and murdered twenty-six people on a Sunday morning, wounding twenty others—ironically on November 5, 2017, the same day that I attended the All Saints Day service at Harris Creek and witnessed the armed-guard. Yet there was no (visible) armed guard at Ebenezer, and the posture and disposition

of the service and its congregation was such that a visibly distraught (and potentially dangerous) individual such as Malchizadek was welcomed there and offered space to speak, to voice his concerns and desires. More than that, it was in the absence of the symbols of power such as a firearm that such a profound musical intervention as the one I witnessed occurred.

Conclusion

1. I draw this idea from the work of Melinda Latour (2016). Latour argues that a category of "moral music" arose in response to the "Wars of Religion" following the initiation of the Protestant Reformation. This musical category was secular, in that it was not sacred, yet it extolled moral virtues that were agreeable to Protestant and Catholic alike and thereby participated in healing relationships and social malaise in that context.

Bibliography

Aksentijevic, Aleksandar, Anthony Smith, and Mark A. Elliott. 2014. "Rate-Specific Entrainment of Harmonic Pitch." *Music Perception: An Interdisciplinary Journal* 31 (4): 316–322. https://doi.org/10.1525/mp.2014.31.4.316.

Alcoff, Linda. 1991. "The Problem of Speaking for Others." *Cultural Critique*, no. 20: 5–32. https://doi.org/10.2307/1354221.

Arndt, Elmer J. F. 1960. "Worship and Ethics in Theology." *Theology and Life* 3 (4): 279.

Auner, Joseph Henry. 2013. *Music in the Twentieth and Twenty-First Centuries*. Western Music in Context: A Norton History. New York: W. W. Norton.

Austin, J. L. 1962. *How to Do Things With Words*. The William James Lectures 1955. Cambridge: Harvard University Press.

Bagnoli, Carla. 2006. Review of *Review of The Ethics of Care: Personal, Political, Global*, by Virginia Held, June. http://ndpr.nd.edu/news/the-ethics-of-care-personal-political-global/.

Balmer, Randall. 2006. *Mine Eyes Have Seen the Glory: A Journey into the Evangelical Subculture in America*, 4th ed. Oxford: Oxford University Press.

Baier, Annette C. 1985. "What Do Women Want in a Moral Theory?" *Noûs* 19 (1): 53–63. https://doi.org/10.2307/2215117.

Baker, Paul. 1985. *Contemporary Christian Music: Where It Came From, What It Is, Where It's Going*. Rev. and expanded ed. Westchester, IL: Crossway Books.

Banner, Michael C. 2016. *The Ethics of Everyday Life: Moral Theology, Social Anthropology, and the Imagination of the Human*. Oxford: Oxford University Press.

Barrett, Lisa Feldman. 2017. *How Emotions Are Made: The Secret Life of the Brain*. Boston: Houghton Mifflin Harcourt.

Bayer, Oswald, and Alan M. Suggate, eds. 1996. *Worship and Ethics: Lutherans and Anglicans in Dialogue*. Theologische Bibliothek Töpelmann, Bd. 70. Berlin: Walter de Gruyter.

Begbie, Jeremy. 2000. *Theology, Music and Time*. Cambridge, UK: Cambridge University Press.

Begbie, Jeremy. 2007. *Resounding Truth: Christian Wisdom in the World of Music*. Engaging Culture. Grand Rapids, MI: Baker Academic.

Begbie, Jeremy. 2011. "Faithful Feelings: Music and Emotion in Worship." In *Resonant Witness: Conversations between Music and Theology*, edited by Steven R. Guthrie and Jeremy S. Begbie, 323–354. Calvin Institute of Christian Worship Liturgical Studies. Grand Rapids, MI: W. B. Eerdmans.

Begbie, Jeremy. 2013. *Music, Modernity, and God: Essays in Listening*. Oxford: Oxford University Press.

Begbie, Jeremy, ed. 2000. *Beholding the Glory: Incarnation through the Arts*. Grand Rapids, MI: Baker Books.

Begbie, Jeremy, and Steven R. Guthrie, eds. 2011. *Resonant Witness: Conversations between Music and Theology*. Calvin Institute of Christian Worship Liturgical Studies. Grand Rapids, MI: W. B. Eerdmans.

Best, Harold. 1993. *Music through the Eyes of Faith*. New York: HarperOne.

Best, Harold M. 2003. *Unceasing Worship: Biblical Perspectives on Worship and the Arts*. Downers Grove, IL: InterVarsity Press.

Bieler, Andrea, and Luise Schottroff. 2007. *The Eucharist: Bodies, Bread, & Resurrection*. Minneapolis, MN: Fortress Press.

Billy, Dennis Joseph, and James Keating. 2006. *The Way of Mystery: The Eucharist and Moral Living*. Mahwah, NJ: Paulist Press.

Bjorlin, David D., and Brent D. Laytham. 2013. "Worship and Ethics: A Selected Bibliography." *Studia liturgica* 43 (1): 169–188.

Black, Rufus. 2001. *Christian Moral Realism*. Oxford: Oxford University Press. http://www.oxfordscholarship.com/view/10.1093/acprof:oso/9780198270201.001.0001/acprof-9780198270201.

Blacking, John. 1974. *How Musical Is Man?* Seattle: University of Washington Press.

Blum, Alan, and Stuart J. Murray, eds. 2017. *The Ethics of Care: Moral Knowledge, Communication, and the Art of Caregiving*. Routledge Studies in Health and Social Welfare 13. Abingdon, UK: Routledge.

Bohman, James, and William Rehg. 2014. "Jürgen Habermas." In *The Stanford Encyclopedia of Philosophy*, edited by Edward N. Zalta, Fall. http://plato.stanford.edu/archives/fall2014/entries/habermas/.

Bohlman, Philip V. 2000. "Ethnomusicology and Music Sociology." In *Musicology and Sister Disciplines*, edited by Greer, David, 288–98. Oxford: Oxford University Press.

Bonhoeffer, Dietrich. 1954. *Life Together*. New York: Harper One.

Bonhoeffer, Dietrich. 1996. *Act and Being: Transcendental Philosophy and Ontology in Systematic Theology*. Translated by Hans-Richard Reuter, Wayne W. Floyd, and Martin Rumscheidt. Dietrich Bonhoeffer Works, vol. 2. Minneapolis, MN: Fortress Press.

Bonhoeffer, Dietrich. 2001. *Discipleship*. Translated by Geffrey B. Kelly and John D. Godsey. Dietrich Bonhoeffer Works, vol. 4. Minneapolis, MN: Fortress Press.

Bonhoeffer, Dietrich. 2005. *Ethics*. Translated by Clifford J. Green, Reinhard Krauss, Charles C. West, and Douglas W. Stott. Dietrich Bonhoeffer Works, vol. 6. Minneapolis, MN: Fortress Press.

Boyd, Todd. 2003. *The New H.N.I.C.: The Death of Civil Rights and the Reign of Hip Hop*. New York: New York University Press. http://public.eblib.com/choice/publicfullrecord.aspx?p=865357.

Boyd, Todd. 2007. *Am I Black Enough for You? Popular Culture from the 'hood and Beyond*. Bloomington: Indiana University Press.

Brabec de Mori, Bernd. 2017. "Music and Non-Human Agency." In *Ethnomusicology: A Contemporary Reader*, vol. 2, edited by Jennifer C. Post, 181–194. Abingdon-on-Thames, UK: Taylor and Francis. http://ebookcentral.proquest.com/lib/bayloru/detail.action?docID=5050755.

Bradley, C. Randall. 2003. "Congregational Song as Shaper of Theology: A Contemporary Assessment." *Review & Expositor* 100 (3): 351–373.

Bradley, C. Randall. 2012. *From Memory to Imagination: Reforming the Church's Music*. Calvin Institute of Christian Worship Liturgical Studies Series. Grand Rapids, MI: W. B. Eerdmans.

Braithwaite, John. 2002. *Restorative Justice & Responsive Regulation*. Oxford: Oxford University Press.

Brooks, Kinitra D., and Kameelah L. Martin. 2019. *The Lemonade Reader: Beyoncé, Black Feminism and Spirituality*. New York: Routledge.

Brown, Frank Burch. 2000. *Good Taste, Bad Taste, & Christian Taste: Aesthetics in Religious Life*. New York: Oxford University Press. http://ezproxy.baylor.edu/login?url=http://dx.doi.org/10.1093/acprof:oso/9780195158724.001.0001.

Brueggemann, Walter. 2001. *Prophetic Imagination*. Rev. ed. Minneapolis, MN: Fortress Press.

Brunk, Timothy M. 2007. *Liturgy and Life: The Unity of Sacrament and Ethics in the Theology of Louis-Marie Chauvet*. American University Studies. Series VII, Theology and Religion, vol. 254. New York: Peter Lang.

Budd, Malcolm. 2002. *Music and the Emotions: The Philosophical Theories*. Abingdon, UK: Routledge.

Burdick, John. 2011. *The Color of Sound: Race, Religion, and Music in Brazil*. New York: New York University Press. http://ezproxy.baylor.edu/login?url=http://www.jstor.org/stable/10.2307/j.ctt9qffrt.

Busman, Joshua Kalin. 2015a. "(Re)Sounding Passion: Listening to American Evangelical Worship Music, 1997–2015." PhD diss., The University of North Carolina at Chapel Hill. http://search.proquest.com/pqdtglobal/docview/1689691201/abstract/FDEBCB23058A4559PQ/60.

Busman, Joshua Kalin. 2015b. "'Yet to Come' or 'Still to Be Done'? Evangelical Worship and the Power of 'Prophetic' Songs." In *Congregational Music-Making and Community in a Mediated Age*, edited by Ann Nekola and Tom Wagner, 199–214. Congregational Music Studies. Farnham, UK: Ashgate.

Caccamo, James Frank. 2004. "The Responsorial Self: Christian Ethics and Ritual Song." PhD diss., Loyola University Chicago. https://search.proquest.com/pqdtglobal/docview/305174000/abstract/B51632716F64407BPQ/1.

Cahill, Lisa Sowle. 1996. *Sex, Gender, and Christian Ethics*. New Studies in Christian Ethics. Cambridge: Cambridge University Press.

Callaway, Kutter. 2013. *Scoring Transcendence: Contemporary Film Music as Religious Experience*. Waco, TX: Baylor University Press.

Cannon, Katie G. 2006. *Black Womanist Ethics*. Eugene, OR: Wipf and Stock Publishers.

Card, Claudia, ed. 1991. *Feminist Ethics*. Lawrence: University Press of Kansas.

Carolyn Boyes-Watson, Susan T. Krumholz, and Aviva M. Rich-Shea. 2013. *Crime and Justice: Learning through Cases*. 2nd ed. Lanham, UK: Rowman & Littlefield.

Cavell, Stanley. 1987. *Disowning Knowledge: In Six Plays of Shakespeare*. Cambridge: Cambridge University Press.

Cavell, Stanley. 1999. *The Claim of Reason: Wittgenstein, Skepticism, Morality, and Tragedy*. Oxford University Press.

Cavell, Stanley. 2004. *Cities of Words: Pedagogical Letters on a Register of the Moral Life*. Cambridge, MA: Belknap Press of Harvard University Press.

Cheng, William. 2016. *Just Vibrations: The Purpose of Sounding Good*. Ann Arbor: University of Michigan Press.

Cheng, William. 2020. *Loving Music Till It Hurts*. Oxford: Oxford University Press.

Childress, James F. 1990. "The Prophetic and the Priestly." *Hastings Center Report* 20 (6): 18.

The Churchman. 1904. n.p.: Churchman.

Clayton, Martin, Rebecca Sager, and Udo Will. 2005. "In Time with the Music: The Concept of Entrainment and Its Significance for Ethnomusicology." *ESEM Counterpoint* 11 (1): 1–82.

Clayton, Martin. 2013. "Entrainment, Ethnography, and Musical Interaction." In *Experience and Meaning in Music Performance*, edited by Martin Clayton, Byron Dueck, and Laura Leante, 19–37. New York: Oxford University Press.

Clifton-Smith, Gregory. 2016. *Performing Pastoral Care: Music as a Framework for Exploring Pastoral Care*. Studies in Religion and Theology. London: Jessica Kingsley.

Cobussen, Marcel, and Nanette Nielsen. 2012. *Music and Ethics*. Farnham, Surrey, UK: Ashgate.

Conradie, Ernst M. 2016. "Is the Ear More Spiritual Than the Eye?" In *Issues in Science and Theology: Do Emotions Shape the World?*, edited by Dirk Evers, Michael Fuller, Anne L. C. Runehov, and Knut-Willy Sæther. European Society for the Study of Science and Theology, vol. 3. New York: Springer.

Cook, Nicholas. 1998. *Analysing Musical Multimedia*. Oxford: Clarendon Press.

Cook, Nicholas. 2014. *Beyond the Score: Music as Performance*. Oxford: Oxford University Press.

Corbitt, J. Nathan. 1998. *The Sound of the Harvest: Music's Mission in Church and Culture*. Grand Rapids, MI: Baker Books.

Crimmins, James E. 2015. "Jeremy Bentham." In *The Stanford Encyclopedia of Philosophy*, edited by Edward N. Zalta, Spring 2015. http://plato.stanford.edu/archives/spr2015/entries/bentham/.

Daly, Mary. 1990. *Gyn/Ecology, the Metaethics of Radical Feminism*. 2nd ed. Boston: Beacon Press.

Darden, Bob. 2004. *People Get Ready! A New History of Black Gospel Music*. London: A&C Black.

Darden, Robert. 2014. *Nothing but Love in God's* Water, vol. 1, *Black Sacred Music from the Civil War to the Civil Rights Movement*. 2 vols. University Park: Pennsylvania State University Press.

Darden, Robert. 2016. *Nothing but Love in God's Water*, vol. 2, *Black Sacred Music from Sit-Ins to Resurrection City*. University Park: Pennsylvania State University Press.

Davies, Eryl W. 1981. "Prophecy and Ethics: Isaiah and the Ethical Traditions of Israel." *Journal for the Study of the Old Testament*. Supplement Series, 16. Sheffield, UK: J.S.O.T. Press.

Davies, Stephen. 1994. *Musical Meaning and Expression*. Ithaca, NY: Cornell University Press.

Davis, Ellen F. 2001. *Getting Involved with God: Rediscovering the Old Testament*. Cambridge, MA: Cowley.

Dawn, Marva J. 1995. *Reaching Out without Dumbing Down: A Theology of Worship for the Turn-of-the-Century Culture*. Grand Rapids, MI: W. B. Eerdmans.

Deleuze, Gilles. 1987. *A Thousand Plateaus: Capitalism and Schizophrenia*. Minneapolis: University of Minnesota Press.

DeNora, Tia. 2011. *Music-in-Action: Selected Essays in Sonic Ecology*. Ashgate Contemporary Thinkers on Critical Musicology. Farnham, UK: Ashgate.

Dickinson, Edward. 1968. *Music in the History of the Western Church*. London: Ardent Media.

Dorrien, Gary J. 2001. *The Making of American Liberal Theology: Imagining Progressive Religion, 1805–1900*. Louisville, KY: Westminster John Knox Press.

Dorrien, Gary J. 2003. *The Making of American Liberal Theology: Idealism, Realism, and Modernity, 1900–1950*. Louisville, KY: Westminster John Knox Press.

Dorrien, Gary J. 2006. *The Making of American Liberal Theology: Crisis, Irony, and Postmodernity 1950–2005*. Louisville, KY: Westminster John Knox Press.

Drösser, Christoph. 2014. "Music and Science: The Goose Bump Effect | TIME ONLINE." ["Musik und Wissenschaft: Der Gänsehaut-Effekt."] *Die Zeit*, April 27, sec. Knowledge. http://www.zeit.de/2010/35/Musik-Wissenschaft.

Dueck, Irma Ruth Fast. 2006. "A Critical Examination of Mennonite Worship and Ethics: A Praxis Approach." ThD diss., Emmanuel College of Victoria University (Canada). http://search.proquest.com/docview/304955972/abstract/667359CF64554D53PQ/1.

Dueck, Jonathan. 2017. *Congregational Music, Conflict, and Community*. New York: Routledge.

Dyson, Michael Eric. 1996. *Between God and Gangsta Rap: Bearing Witness to Black Culture*. New York: Oxford University Press.

Engelhardt, Jeffers. 2015. *Singing the Right Way: Orthodox Christians and Secular Enchantment in Estonia*. Oxford: Oxford University Press.

Epstein, Heidi. 2004. *Melting the Venusberg: A Feminist Theology of Music*. New York: Continuum.

Eugene, Toinette M. 1992. "On 'Difference' and the Dream of Pluralist Feminism." *Journal of Feminist Studies in Religion* 8 (2): 91–98.

Evers, Dirk, Michael Fuller, Anne L. C. Runehov, Knut-Willy Stæher, and ebrary, Inc., eds. 2016. *Issues in Science and Theology: Do Emotions Shape the World?* European Society for the Study of Science and Theology, vol. 3. New York: Springer.

Fabbri, Franco. 1982. "A Theory of Musical Genres: Two Applications." *Popular Music Perspectives* 1: 52–81.

Farley, Margaret A. 2002. *Compassionate Respect: A Feminist Approach to Medical Ethics and Other Questions*. Madeleva Lecture in Spirituality 2002. New York: Paulist Press.

Faulkner, Quentin. 1996. *Wiser Than Despair: The Evolution of Ideas in the Relationship of Music and the Christian Church*. Contributions to the Study of Music and Dance, no. 40. Westport, CN: Greenwood Press.

Feld, Steven, and Aaron A. Fox. 1994. "Music and Language." *Annual Review of Anthropology* 23: 25–53.

Feld, Steven, and Aaron Fox. 1999. "Music." *Journal of Linguistic Anthropology* 9 (1/2): 159–162.

Felix-Jager, Steven. 2017. *With God on Our Side: Towards a Transformational Theology of Rock and Roll*. Eugene, OR: Wipf & Stock.

Ferguson, Todd W. 2016. "Gender and Status in the Religious Congregation." PhD diss., Baylor University. https://search-proquest-com.ezproxy.baylor.edu/docview/1803936930/ADEB17B38D5A4C61PQ/1.

Floyd, Samuel A. Jr. 1996. *The Power of Black Music: Interpreting Its History from Africa to the United States*. New York: Oxford University Press.

Ford, Tanisha C. 2019. "Beysthetics: 'Formation' and the Politics of Style." In *The Lemonade Reader: Beyoncé, Black Feminism and Spirituality*, edited by Kinitra D. Brooks and Kameelah L. Martin, 192–199. New York: Routledge.

Foucault, Michel. 1983. *Ceci n'est pas une Pipe (This Is Not a Pipe)*. Translated by James Harkness. Berkeley: University of California Press.

Foucault, Michel. 1984. *The Foucault Reader*. Edited by Paul Rabinow. New York: Pantheon Books.

Foucault, Michel, Mauro Bertani, Alessandro Fontana, François Ewald, and David Macey. 2003. *Society Must Be Defended: Lectures at the Collège de France, 1975–76*. New York: Picador.

Foucault, Michel, Paul Rabinow, Robert Hurley, James D. Faubion, and Michel Foucault. 1997a. *The Essential Works of Michel Foucault, 1954–1984*. New York: New Press; distributed by W.W. Norton.

———. 1997b. *The Essential Works of Michel Foucault, 1954–1984: Aesthetics, Method, and Epistemology*. New York: New Press; distributed by W.W. Norton.

———. 1997c. *The Essential Works of Michel Foucault, 1954–1984: Ethics*, vol. 1, *Subjectivity and Truth*. New York: New Press; distributed by W.W. Norton.

———. 1997d. *The Essential Works of Michel Foucault, 1954–1984: Power*. New York: New Press; distributed by W.W. Norton.

Frame, John M. 1997. *Contemporary Worship Music: A Biblical Defense*. Phillipsburg, NJ: P&R.

Friedman, Marilyn. 1995. "Beyond Caring: The De-Moralization of Gender." In *Justice and Care: Essential Readings in Feminist Ethics*, edited by Virginia Held, 61–78. Boulder, CO: Westview Press.

Frith, Simon. 1989. "Why Do Songs Have Words?" *Contemporary Music Review* 5 (1): 77–96. https://doi.org/10.1080/07494468900640551.

Frith, Simon. 1996. *Performing Rites: On the Value of Popular Music*. Oxford: Oxford University Press.

Fultz, Daniel D. 2010. "Style Matters: Worship Preferences of University Students Regarding the Use of Music and Technology." PhD. diss., Bowling Green State University.

Funk, Robert W. 1964. "'How Do You Read?' A Sermon on Luke 10: 25–37." *Union Seminary Magazine* 18 (1): 56–61.

Gammage, Marquita. 2017. "Pop Culture without Culture: Examining the Public Backlash to Beyoncé's Super Bowl 50 Performance." *Journal of Black Studies* 48 (8): 715–731. https://doi.org/10.1177/0021934717729504.

Gell, Alfred. 1998. *Art and Agency: An Anthropological Theory*. New York: Clarendon Press.

Gerald C., Liu. 2017. *Music and the Generosity of God*. Radical Theologies and Philosophies 14521. New York: Palgrave Macmillan.

Gibson, James J. 1979. *The Ecological Approach to Visual Perception*. Boston: Houghton Mifflin.

Gilligan, Carol. 1982. *In a Different Voice: Psychological Theory and Women's Development*. 2nd ed. Cambridge, MA: Harvard University Press.

Goleman, Daniel. 2006. *Emotional Intelligence*. New York: Bantam Books.

Goodman, Steve. 2010. *Sonic Warfare: Sound, Affect, and the Ecology of Fear*. Technologies of Lived Abstraction. Cambridge, MA: MIT Press.

Gupta, Nijay K. 2010. *Worship That Makes Sense to Paul: A New Approach to the Theology and Ethics of Paul's Cultic Metaphors*. Beihefte Zur Zeitschrift Für Die Neutestamentliche Wissenschaft Und Die Kunde Der Älteren Kirche, Bd. 175. Berlin: De Gruyter.

Guroian, Vigen. 1985. "Seeing Worship as Ethics: An Orthodox Perspective." *Journal of Religious Ethics* 13 (2): 332–359.

Gustafson, James M. 1961. *Treasure in Earthen Vessels: The Church as a Human Community*. New York: Harper.

Gustafson, James M. 1981. *Ethics from a Theocentric Perspective*. Chicago: University of Chicago Press.

Gyure, Joseph. 2009. "Waco History Project: I35." http://wacohistoryproject.org/Places/I35.htm.

Habermas, Jürgen. 1990. *Moral Consciousness and Communicative Action*. Translated by Christian Lenhardt and Shierry Weber Nicholsen. Studies in Contemporary German Social Thought. Cambridge, MA: MIT Press.

Hamilton, Michael S. 1999. "The Triumph of Praise Songs: How Guitars Beat Out the Organ in the Worship Wars." *Christianity Today* (July 12).

Haste, Amanda Jane. 2016. "Conflict and Reparation: The Agency of Music in Modern Monastic Community Dynamics." *Music and Arts in Action* 5 (2): 39–54. http://www.musicandartsinaction.net/index.php/maia/article/view/123.

Hauerwas, Stanley. 2015a. *The Work of Theology*. Grand Rapids, MI: W. B. Eerdmans.

Hauerwas, Stanley. 2015b. *Performing the Faith: Bonhoeffer and the Practice of Nonviolence*. Eugene, OR: Wipf and Stock.

Hauerwas, Stanley, Samuel Wells, and ebrary, Inc, eds. 2011. *The Blackwell Companion to Christian Ethics*. 2nd ed. Blackwell Companions to Religion. Malden, MA: Wiley-Blackwell. http://ezproxy.baylor.edu/login?url=http://site.ebrary.com/lib/baylor/docDetail.action?docID=10510567.

Hauerwas, Stanley, and William H. Willimon. 1989. *Resident Aliens: Life in the Christian Colony*. Nashville, TN: Abingdon Press.

Hawn, C. Michael. 2003a. *Gather into One: Praying and Singing Globally*. Grand Rapids, MI: W. B. Eerdmans.

Hawn, C. Michael. 2003b. *One Bread, One Body: Exploring Cultural Diversity in Worship*. New York: Rowman & Littlefield.

Hawn, C. Michael, and James Abbington, eds. 2013. *New Songs of Celebration Render: Congregational Song in the Twenty-First Century*. Chicago, IL: GIA.

Hays, Christopher M. 2016. *When the Son of Man Didn't Come: A Constructive Proposal on the Delay of the Parousia*. Minneapolis, MN: Fortress Press.

Hefley, James C. 1991. *The Conservative Resurgence in the Southern Baptist Convention*. n.p.: Hannibal Books.

Heidegger, Martin, and Joan Stambaugh. 1996. *Being and Time: A Translation of Sein und Zeit*. SUNY Series in Contemporary Continental Philosophy. Albany: State University of New York Press.

Held, Virginia, ed. 1995. *Justice and Care: Essential Readings in Feminist Ethics*. Boulder, CO: Westview Press.

Held, Virginia. 2006. *The Ethics of Care: Personal, Political, and Global*. Oxford University Press.

Hesmondhalgh, David. 2013. *Why Music Matters*. Chichester, West Sussex, UK: Wiley Blackwell.

Hicks, Zac M. 2016. *The Worship Pastor: A Call to Ministry for Worship Leaders and Teams*. Grand Rapids, MI: Zondervan.

Higgins, Kathleen Marie. 1991. *The Music of Our Lives*. Philadelphia: Temple University Press.

Hirschkind, Charles. 2006. *The Ethical Soundscape: Cassette Sermons and Islamic Counterpublics*. New York: Columbia University Press. http://public.eblib.com/choice/publicfullrecord.aspx?p=908454.

Hoagland, Sarah Lucia. 1991. "Some Thoughts about 'Caring.'" In *Feminist Ethics*, edited by Claudia Card, 246–264. Lawrence: University Press of Kansas.

Holder, Arthur. 2011. *The Blackwell Companion to Christian Spirituality*. De Kalb, IL: John Wiley. http://books.google.com/books?hl=en&lr=&id=4-KvM69hyCMC&oi=fnd&pg=PR8&dq=%22%C2%A9+2011.+Wiley-Blackwell.+All+rights%22+%22companions+to+religion+:+Blackwell+Companion+to+Christian+Ethics+(2).+Hoboken,+GB:+Wiley-Blackwell,+2011.+ProQuest+ebrary.+Web.+18+October%22+%22%C2%A9+2011.+Wiley-Blackwell.+All+rights%22+&ots=__z79c2_zi&sig=wSW9QeY24meXwUK3Elm27TD5xnI.

Holt, Fabian. 2007. *Genre in Popular Music*. Chicago: University of Chicago Press.

Hunt, Mary E., Emilie M. Townes, and Ellen M. Umansky. 1992. "Respondents." *Journal of Feminist Studies in Religion* 8 (2): 110–122.

Hursthouse, Rosalind. 2013. "Virtue Ethics." In *The Stanford Encyclopedia of Philosophy*, edited by Edward N. Zalta, Fall. http://plato.stanford.edu/archives/fall2013/entries/ethics-virtue/.

Hustad, Don. 1993. *Jubilate II: Church Music in Worship and Renewal*. Carol Stream, IL: Hope.

Ingalls, Monique. 2008. "Awesome in This Place: Sound, Space, and Identity in Contemporary North American Evangelical Worship." PhD diss., University of Pennsylvania. http://search.proquest.com.ezproxy.baylor.edu/docview/304494371/abstract/667024D74C684480PQ/3.

Ingalls, Monique. 2011. "Singing Heaven Down to Earth: Spiritual Journeys, Eschatological Sounds, and Community Formation in Evangelical Conference Worship." *Ethnomusicology* 55 (2): 255–279.

Ingalls, Monique. 2012. "Contemporary Worship Music." In *Continuum Encyclopedia of Popular Music of the World*, vol. 8, *Genres, North America*. London: Continuum.

Ingalls, Monique. 2014. "International Gospel and Christian Music." In *Bloomsbury Encyclopedia of Popular Music of the World*, vol. 9. https://333sound.com/2014/06/09/epmow-vol-9-gospel-and-christian-popular-music/.

Ingalls, Monique. 2017. "Style Matters: Contemporary Worship Music and the Meaning of Popular Musical Borrowings." *Liturgy* 32 (1): 7–15. https://doi.org/10.1080/0458063X.2016.1229435.

Ingalls, Monique. 2018. *Singing the Congregation: How Contemporary Worship Music Forms Evangelical Community*. Oxford: Oxford University Press.

Ingalls, Monique, Carolyn Landau, and Thomas Wagner, eds. 2013. *Christian Congregational Music: Performance, Identity, and Experience*. Farnham, Surrey: Ashgate Publishing Limited.

Ingalls, Monique, and Amos Yong, eds. 2015. *The Spirit of Praise: Music and Worship in Global Pentecostal-Charismatic Christianity*. University Park: Pennsylvania State University Press.

Isasi-Díaz, Ada María. 1992. "Viva La Diferencia!" *Journal of Feminist Studies in Religion* 8 (2): 98–102.

Isasi-Díaz, Ada María. 2004. *En La Lucha = In the Struggle: Elaborating a Mujerista Theology*. Minneapolis, MN: Fortress Press.

Jaggar, Alison M. 1995. "Caring as a Feminist Practice of Moral Reason." In *Justice and Care: Essential Readings in Feminist Ethics*, edited by Virginia Held, 179–202. Boulder, CO: Westview Press.

Johansson, Calvin M. 1984. *Music & Ministry: A Biblical Counterpoint*. Peabody, MA: Hendrickson.

Johansson, Calvin M. 1992. *Discipling Music Ministry*. Peabody, MA: Hendrickson.

John Coleman. 2000. "How the Eucharist Proclaims Social Justice, Pt 1." *Church* 16, 5–9.

John Coleman. 2001. "How the Eucharist Proclaims Social Justice, Pt 2." *Church* 17, 11–15.

Johnson, Bruce, and Martin Cloonan. 2008. *Dark Side of the Tune: Popular Music and Violence*. Ashgate Popular and Folk Music Series. Burlington, VT: Ashgate.

Johnson, Todd E., ed. 2002. *The Conviction of Things Not Seen: Worship and Ministry in the 21st Century*. Grand Rapids, MI: Brazos Press.

Johnson, Todd E., and Dale Savidge. 2009. *Performing the Sacred (Engaging Culture): Theology and Theatre in Dialogue*. Grand Rapids, MI: Baker Academic.

Johnstone, Gerry, and Daniel Van Ness. 2013. *Handbook of Restorative Justice*. Abingdon, UK: Routledge.

Juslin, Patrik N., and John Sloboda. 2011. *Handbook of Music and Emotion: Theory, Research, Applications*. Oxford University Press.

Justice, Deborah R. 2012. "Sonic Change, Social Change, Sacred Change: Music and the Reconfiguration of American Christianity." PhD, Indiana University. http://search.proquest.com.ezproxy.baylor.edu/pqdtglobal/docview/1037812173/abstract/E2CDA6C82DBB43D1PQ/1.

Justice, Deborah R. 2017. "The Curious Longevity of the Traditional–Contemporary Divide: Mainline Musical Choices in Post–Worship War America." *Liturgy* 32 (1): 16–23. https://doi.org/10.1080/0458063X.2016.1229438.

Kadushin, Max. 1964. *Worship and Ethics, a Study in Rabbinic Judaism*. Evanston, IL: Northwestern University Press.

Kaylor, Brian. 2015. *Sacramental Politics: Religious Worship as Political Action*. Frontiers in Political Communication, vol. 30. New York: Peter Lang.

Keljo, Kurt. 2000. "Liturgy and the Moral Self: Humanity at Full Stretch before God." *Journal of Moral Education* 29 (2): 232.

Keltner, Dacher, Deborah H. Gruenfeld, and Cameron Anderson. 2003. "Power, Approach, and Inhibition." *Psychological Review* 110 (2): 265–284. https://doi.org/10.1037/0033-295X.110.2.265.

Kemper, Theodore D. 2011. *Status, Power and Ritual Interaction: A Relational Reading of Durkheim, Goffman, and Collins*. Farnham, Surrey, UK: Ashgate. http://ezproxy.baylor.edu/login?url=http://site.ebrary.com/lib/baylor/Top?id=10490676.

Kivy, Peter. 2002. *Introduction to a Philosophy of Music*. Oxford: Oxford University Press.

Kivy, Peter. 2007. *Music, Language, and Cognition: And Other Essays in the Aesthetics of Music*. Oxford: Oxford University Press.

Kleef, Gerben A. van, Christopher Oveis, Ilmo van der Löwe, Aleksandr LuoKogan, Jennifer Goetz, and Dacher Keltner. 2008. "Power, Distress, and Compassion: Turning a Blind Eye to the Suffering of Others." *Psychological Science* 19 (12): 1315–1322. https://doi.org/10.1111/j.1467-9280.2008.02241.x.

Labbe, C., and D. Grandjean. 2014. "Musical Emotions Predicted by Feelings of Entrainment." *Music Perception: An Interdisciplinary Journal* 32 (2): 170–185. https://doi.org/10.1525/mp.2014.32.2.170.

Lakies, Chad. 2013. "Foucault and Bonhoeffer on the Power of Confession for the Soul." In "The Soul" Conference. Oxford University, UK. https://www.academia.edu/9679523/Foucault_and_Bonhoeffer_on_the_Power_of_Confession_for_the_Soul.

Lemons, J. Derrick, ed. 2018. *Theologically Engaged Anthropology*. Oxford: Oxford University Press.

Lévinas, Emmanuel. 1998. *Otherwise Than Being, or, Beyond Essence*. Pittsburgh, PA: Duquesne University Press.

Lévinas, Emmanuel. 1999. *Alterity and Transcendence*. European Perspectives. New York: Columbia University Press.

Lévinas, Emmanuel. 2000. *Totality and Infinity: An Essay on Exteriority*. Translated by Alphonso Lingis. Pittsburgh, PA: Duquesne University Press.

Lévinas, Emmanuel, and Bettina Bergo. 2000. *God, Death, and Time*. Meridian. Stanford, CA: Stanford University Press.

Lévinas, Emmanuel, Philippe Nemo, and Richard A. Cohen. 1985. *Ethics and Infinity*. Pittsburgh, PA: Duquesne University Press.

Lévinas, Emmanuel, Michael B. Smith, and Barbara Harshav. 1998. *Entre Nous: On Thinking-of-the-Other*. European Perspectives. New York: Columbia University Press.

Levinson, Jerrold. 1990. *Music, Art, and Metaphysics: Essays in Philosophical Aesthetics*. Ithaca, NY: Cornell University Press. https://catalog.hathitrust.org/Record/002444937.

Levitin, Daniel J. 2007. *This Is Your Brain on Music: The Science of a Human Obsession*, 1 Reprint ed. New York, NY: Plume/Penguin.

Lim, Swee Hong, and Lester Ruth. 2017. *Lovin' on Jesus: A Concise History of Contemporary Worship*. Nashville, TN: Abingdon Press.

Lipsitz, George. 2018. *The Possessive Investment in Whiteness: How White People Profit from Identity Politics*, 20th anniversary ed. Philadelphia, PA: Temple University Press.
Lorde, Audre. 2015. "An Open Letter to Mary Daly; The Master's Tools Will Never Dismantle the Master's House." In *This Bridge Called My Back: Writings by Radical Women of Color*, 4th ed., edited by Cherríe Moraga and Gloria Anzaldúa, 90–97. Albany: State University of New York Press.
Love, Nancy Sue. 2006. *Musical Democracy*. Albany: State University of New York Press.
Lovelace, Austin C., and William C. Rice. 1976. *Music and Worship in the Church*. Rev. and enlarged ed. Nashville, TN: Abingdon.
MacIntyre, Alasdair C. 1978. *Against the Self-Images of the Age: Essays on Ideology and Philosophy*. Notre Dame, IN: University of Notre Dame Press.
MacIntyre, Alasdair C. 1984. *After Virtue: A Study in Moral Theory*. 2nd ed. Notre Dame, IN: University of Notre Dame Press.
Mall, Andrew. 2015. "'We Can Be Renewed': Resistance and Worship at the Anchor Fellowship." In *The Spirit of Praise: Music and Worship in Global Pentecostal-Charismatic Christianity*, edited by Monique Marie Ingalls and Amos Yong, 163–178. University Park: Pennsylvania State University Press.
Mall, Andrew. 2020. *God Rock, Inc.* Berkeley, CA: University of California Press.
Margulis, Elizabeth Hellmuth. 2014. *On Repeat: How Music Plays the Mind*. New York: Oxford University Press.
Mayer, John D., and Glenn Geher. 1996. "Emotional Intelligence and the Identification of Emotion." *Intelligence* 22 (2): 89–113. https://doi.org/10.1016/S0160-2896(96)90011-2.
McClary, Susan. 2002. *Feminine Endings: Music, Gender, and Sexuality*. Reprint. Minneapolis: University of Minnesota Press.
McGann, Mary E. 2002. *Exploring Music as Worship and Theology: Research in Liturgical Practice*. American Essays in Liturgy. Collegeville, MN: Liturgical Press.
McNelis, Tim. 2017. *US Youth Films and Popular Music: Identity, Genre, and Musical Agency*. Routledge Advances in Film Studies 53. New York: Routledge.
Meier-Oeser, Stephan. 2011. "Medieval Semiotics." In *The Stanford Encyclopedia of Philosophy*, edited by Edward N. Zalta, Summer 2011. http://plato.stanford.edu/archives/sum2011/entries/semiotics-medieval/.
Meyer, Leonard B. 1956. *Emotion and Meaning in Music*. University of Chicago Press.
Mitchell, Philip Irving. ND. "An Overview of the Ethics of Dietrich Bonhoeffer." Academic Institution, Faculty Blog. Dallas Baptist University. http://www3.dbu.edu/mitchell/bonhoefferethics.htm.
Mitchell, Robert H. 1978. *Ministry and Music*. Philadelphia: Westminster Press.
Mohanty, Chandra Talpade. 1988. "Under Western Eyes: Feminist Scholarship and Colonial Discourses." *Feminist Review*, no. 30: 61–88. https://doi.org/10.2307/1395054.
Moody-Adams, Michele M. 1991. "Gender and the Complexity of Moral Voice." In *Feminist Ethics*, edited by Claudia Card, 195–212. Lawrence: University Press of Kansas.
Moore, Allan F. 2001. "Categorical Conventions in Music Discourse: Style and Genre." *Music & Letters* 82 (3): 432–442.
Moore, Allan F. 2015. "On the Inherent Contradiction in Worship Music." In *Congregational Music-Making and Community in a Mediated Age*, edited by Anna E. Nekola and Tom Wagner. Congregational Music Studies. Farnham, UK: Ashgate.
Moore, Marissa Glynias. 2017. "Treating the 'Other' as a 'Thou': Recontextualization and the Search for Origins in Global Song Transmission." *The Hymn* 68 (1): 9–15.

Moser, Stan. 2015. *We Will Stand*. Brentwood, TN: CCM United.

Müller, B. A. 2006. "The Role of Worship and Ethics on the Road towards Reconciliation." *Verbum et Ecclesia* 27 (2): 641–663.

Murphy, Kevin R., ed. 2006. *A Critique of Emotional Intelligence: What Are the Problems and How Can They Be Fixed?* Series in Applied Psychology. Mahwah, NJ: Lawrence Erlbaum.

Music, David W. 2008. *Music and Worship: The Emerging Experiences of Baptists*. Atlanta, GA: Baptist Heritage Society.

Music, David W., ed. 1998. *Instruments in Church: A Collection of Source Documents*. Studies in Liturgical Musicology, no. 7. Lanham, MD: Scarecrow Press.

Myrick, Nathan. 2014. "An Honest Question to Difficult Answers: Explorations in Music, Culturalism, and Reconciliation." *Liturgy* 29 (3): 37–46. https://doi.org/10.1080/0458063X.2014.894831.

Myrick, Nathan. 2015. "The Ethics of Normativity and Exclusion: Sexual Orientation and Acceptance by Musical Genre." In *Bi-Annual Meeting of the Christian Congregational Music Conference*. Oxfordshire, UK.

Myrick, Nathan. 2017. "Relational Power, Music, and Identity: The Emotional Efficacy of Congregational Song." *Yale Journal of Music & Religion* 3 (1): 77–92. https://doi.org/10.17132/2377-231X.1060.

Myrick, Nathan. 2018a. "Double Authenticity: Celebrity, Consumption, and the Christian Worship Music Industry." *The Hymn* 69 (2): 21–27.

Myrick, Nathan. 2018b. "The Art of Listening in Multicultural Worship." *The Hymn* 69 (4): 35–36.

Myrick, Nathan. 2018c. "The Celebrity Model of Music Ministry: Characteristics and Considerations." *The Hymn* 69 (3): 23–26.

Myrick, Nathan, and Mark Porter, eds. Forthcoming. *Ethics and Christian Musicking*. Congregational Music Studies Series. New York: Routledge.

Nekola, Anna E. 2009. "Between This World and the Next: The Musical 'Worship Wars' and Evangelical Ideology in the United States, 1960–2005." PhD diss., University of Wisconsin-Madison. http://search.proquest.com/pqdtglobal/docview/305033619/abstract/F455AD76D32041BAPQ/19.

Nekola, Anna E. 2015. "Negotiating the Tensions of U.S. Worship Music in the Marketplace." In *Oxford Handbooks Online*, edited by Jonathan Dueck and Suzel Ana Reily, Oxford Handbook of Music and World Christianities, 513–529. http://www.academia.edu/download/44004642/Ingalls_2013_-__Transnational_Connections.pdf.

Nekola, Anna E., and Tom Wagner, eds. 2015. *Congregational Music-Making and Community in a Mediated Age*. Congregational Music Studies. Farnham, UK: Ashgate.

Niebuhr, H. Richard. 1956. *Christ and Culture*. New York: Harper.

Niebuhr, H. Richard. 1960. *The Meaning of Revelation*. New York: Macmillan.

Niebuhr, H. Richard. 1963. *The Responsible Self: An Essay in Christian Moral Philosophy*. New York: Harper & Row.

Niebuhr, Reinhold. 1949. *Faith and History: A Comparison of Christian and Modern Views of History*. New York: C. Scribner's Sons.

Niebuhr, Reinhold. 1955. *The Self and the Dramas of History*. New York: Scribner.

Niebuhr, Reinhold. 1971. *Beyond Tragedy; Essays on the Christian Interpretation of History*. Essay Index Reprint Series. Freeport, NY: Books for Libraries Press.

Niebuhr, Reinhold. 1979. *An Interpretation of Christian Ethics*. New York: Seabury Press.

Niebuhr, H. Richard, and Kristine A. Culp. 2008. *"The Responsibility of the Church for Society" and Other Essays by H. Richard Niebuhr*. Library of Theological Ethics. Louisville, KY: Westminster John Knox Press.

Noddings, Nel. 2013. *Caring: A Feminine Approach to Ethics & Moral Education*. 3rd ed. Berkeley: University of California Press.

Nussbaum, Martha. 2002. "Capabilities and Social Justice." *International Studies Review* 4 (2): 123–135.

Nussbaum, Martha. 2011. *Creating Capabilities: The Human Development Approach*. Cambridge, MA: Belknap Press of Harvard University Press.

Nussbaum, Martha Craven. 2001. *Upheavals of Thought: The Intelligence of Emotions*. Cambridge: Cambridge University Press.

O'Brien, Melinda Anne Latour. 2016. "Music and Moral Repair in Early Modern France." PhD diss., University of California, Los Angeles. http://search.proquest.com.ezproxy.baylor.edu/pqdtglobal/docview/1795076259/abstract/D0FF38D392974961PQ/1.

Okin, Susan Moller. 1994. "Political Liberalism, Justice, and Gender." *Ethics* 105 (1): 23–43.

Partridge, Christopher H. 2017. "Emotion, Meaning and Popular Music." In *The Bloomsbury Handbook of Religion and Popular Music*, edited by Christopher H. Partridge and Marcus Moberg, 23–31. Bloomsbury Handbooks in Religion. London: Bloomsbury Academic.

Partridge, Christopher, and Marcus Moberg. 2017. *The Bloomsbury Handbook of Religion and Popular Music*. London: Bloomsbury Academic.

Pellitteri, John, Robin Stern, and Luba Nakhutina. 1999. "Music: The Sounds of Emotional Intelligence." *Voices from the Middle; Urbana* 7 (1): 25–29.

Pembroke, Neil. 2010. *Pastoral Care in Worship: Liturgy and Psychology in Dialogue*. London: T & T Clark.

Percy, Martyn. 1996. *Words, Wonders and Power: Understanding Contemporary Christian Fundamentalism and Revivalism*. London: S.P.C.K.

Perez, Adam. 2018. "Contemporary Worship Music and Everyday Musical Lives (Mark Porter)." *Global Forum on Arts and Christian Faith* (6): 323–326. http://artsandchristianfaith.org/index.php/journal/article/view/49.

Peters, Ted. 1994. "Worship Wars: Battling on Four Fronts." *Dialog* 33 (3): 166–73.

Peterson, Brent D. 2012. *Created to Worship: God's Invitation to Become Fully Human*. Kansas City, MO: Beacon Hill Press of Kansas City. http://public.eblib.com/choice/publicfullrecord.aspx?p=3379570.

Phillips, Elizabeth. 2012. "Charting the 'Ethnographic Turn': Theologians and the Study of Christian Congregations." In *Perspectives on Ecclesiology and Ethnography*, edited by Pete Ward, 95–106. Studies in Ecclesiology and Ethnography. Grand Rapids, MI: W. B. Eerdmans.

Phillips, Wesley. 2015. *Metaphysics and Music in Adorno and Heidegger*. New York: Palgrave Macmillan.

Plaskow, Judith. 1992. "Appropriation, Reciprocity, and Issues of Power." *Journal of Feminist Studies in Religion* 8 (2): 105–110.

Porter, Mark James. 2014. "That's Not My Music: Experiences of Contemporary Worship Music in Relation to Extraecclesiastical Musical Attachments." PhD diss., City University, London.

Porter, Mark James. 2016. *Contemporary Worship Music and Everyday Musical Lives*. Ashgate Congregational Music Studies Series. New York: Routledge.

Post, Jennifer C. 2017. *Ethnomusicology: A Contemporary Reader*, vol. 2. New York: Taylor and Francis. http://ebookcentral.proquest.com/lib/bayloru/detail.action?docID=5050755.

Pound, Pandora, and Rona Campbell. 2015. "Exploring the Feasibility of Theory Synthesis: A Worked Example in the Field of Health Related Risk-Taking." *Social Science & Medicine* 124 (January): 57–65. https://doi.org/10.1016/j.socscimed.2014.11.029.

Pui-lan, Kwok. 1992. "Speaking from the Margins." *Journal of Feminist Studies in Religion* 8 (2): 102–105.

Purcell, Michael. 1997. "Created to Worship: The Invitation to Become Fully Human." *Heythrop Journal* 38: 144–164.

Quine, W. V., Dagfinn Føllesdal, and Douglas B. Quine. 2008. *Confessions of a Confirmed Extensionalist: And Other Essays*. Cambridge, MA: Harvard University Press.

Quine, W. V., and J. S. Ullian. 1978. *The Web of Belief*. 2nd ed. New York: Random House.

Rauschenbusch, Walter. 1907. *Christianity and the Social Crisis in the 21st Century: The Classic That Woke Up the Church*. New York: Zondervan.

Rawls, John. 1999. *A Theory of Justice*. Rev. ed. Cambridge, MA: Belknap Press of Harvard University Press.

Resnicow, Joel E., Peter Salovey, and Bruno H. Repp. 2004. "Is Recognition of Emotion in Music Performance an Aspect of Emotional Intelligence?" *Music Perception: An Interdisciplinary Journal* 22 (1): 145–158. https://doi.org/10.1525/mp.2004.22.1.145.

Rienstra, Debra K., and Ron Rienstra. n.d. *Worship Words: Discipling Language for Faithful Ministry*.

Riethmüller, Albrecht. 2008. "Music beyond Ethics." *Archiv Für Musikwissenschaft* 65 (3): 169–176.

Rinderle, Peter. 2011. *Musik, Emotionen und Ethik*. Freiburg im Breisgau: Verlag Herder GmbH.

Roberts, Robert Campbell. 2007. *Spiritual Emotions: A Psychology of Christian Virtues*. Grand Rapids, MI: W. B. Eerdmans.

Robinson, Fiona. 2011. *The Ethics of Care: A Feminist Approach to Human Security*. Global Ethics and Politics. Philadelphia, PA: Temple University Press. http://ezproxy.baylor.edu/login?url=http://www.jstor.org/stable/10.2307/j.ctt14bt8bq.

Robison B. James, Gary H. Leazer, and James Shoopman. 1999. *The Fundamentalist Takeover in the Southern Baptist Convention: A Brief History*. n.p.: Impact Media.

Rohlf, Michael. 2016. "Immanuel Kant." In *The Stanford Encyclopedia of Philosophy*, edited by Edward N. Zalta, Spring 2016. http://plato.stanford.edu/archives/spr2016/entries/kant/.

Rojek, Chris. 2015. "Celebrity." In *The Wiley Blackwell Encyclopedia of Consumption and Consumer Studies*. New York: John Wiley. https://doi.org/10.1002/9781118989463.wbeccs036, 10.1002/9781118989463.wbeccs036.

Rommen, Timothy. 2007. *"Mek Some Noise": Gospel Music and the Ethics of Style in Trinidad*. Music of the African Diaspora 11. Berkeley: University of California Press.

Rossi, Philip J. 1979. "Narrative, Worship, and Ethics: Empowering Images for the Shape of Christian Moral Life." *Journal of Religious Ethics* 7 (2): 239–248.

Routley, Erik. 1967. *Music Leadership in the Church*. Nashville, TN: Abingdon Press.

Routley, Erik. 1978. *Church Music and the Christian Faith*. Carol Stream, IL: Agape.

Ruddick, Sara. 1995a. "Injustice in Families: Assault and Domination." In *Justice and Care: Essential Readings in Feminist Ethics*, edited by Virginia Held. Boulder, CO: Westview Press.

Ruddick, Sara. 1995b. *Maternal Thinking: Toward a Politics of Peace*. Boston, MA: Beacon Press.

Ruth, Lester. 2000. *A Little Heaven Below*. Nashville, TN: Abingdon Press.

Ruth, Lester. 2010. *Walking Where Jesus Walked: Worship in Fourth-Century Jerusalem*. Grand Rapids, MI: W. B. Eerdmans.

Ruth, Lester. 2017a. "The Eruption of Worship Wars: The Coming of Conflict." *Liturgy* 32 (1): 3–6. https://doi.org/10.1080/0458063X.2016.1229431.

Ruth, Lester. 2017b. "Worship in an Age of Reconstruction: Introduction." *Liturgy* 32 (1): 1–2. https://doi.org/10.1080/0458063X.2016.1229428.

Sacks, Oliver. 2008. *Musicophilia: Tales of Music and the Brain*. Rev. and enlarged ed. New York: Vintage.

Sagavsky, Nicholas. 2005. "Review of 'Political Worship: Ethics for Christian Citizens' by Bernd Wannenwetsch." *New Blackfriars* 86 (1004): 460–461.

Saliers, D. E. 1979. "Liturgy and Ethics: Some New Beginnings." *Journal of Religious Ethics* 7 (2): 173–189.

Saliers, Don E. 1980. *The Soul in Paraphrase: Prayer and the Religious Affections*. New York: Seabury Press.

Saliers, Don E. 1994. *Worship as Theology: Foretaste of Glory Divine*. Nashville, TN: Abingdon.

Saliers, Don E. 2007. *Music and Theology*. Nashville, TN: Abingdon Press.

Saliers, Don E., E. Byron Anderson, and Bruce T. Morrill. 1998. *Liturgy and the Moral Self: Humanity at Full Stretch Before God: Essays in Honor of Don E. Saliers*. Minneapolis, MN: Liturgical Press.

Salovey, Peter, and John D. Mayer. 1990. "Emotional Intelligence." *Imagination, Cognition and Personality* 9 (3): 185–211. https://doi.org/10.2190/DUGG-P24E-52WK-6CDG.

Sayres, Alfred. 1961. "Worship and Ethics in the Ministry." *Theology and Life* 4 (1): 37–47.

Schellenberg, E. Glenn. 2011. "Music Lessons, Emotional Intelligence, and IQ." *Music Perception; Berkeley* 29 (2): 185–194.

Scharen, Christian B., ed. 2012. *Explorations in Ecclesiology and Ethnography*. Grand Rapids, MI: W. B. Eerdmans.

Scharen, Christian B., and Aana Marie Vigen, eds. 2011. *Ethnography as Christian Theology and Ethics*. London: Continuum.

Seasoltz, R. Kevin. 2012. *A Virtuous Church: Catholic Theology, Ethics, and Liturgy for the 21st Century*. Maryknoll, NY: Orbis Books.

Slote, Michael. 2007. *The Ethics of Care and Empathy*. London: Routledge.

Small, Christopher. 1998. *Musicking: The Meanings of Performing and Listening*. Music/Culture. Hanover, NH: University Press of New England.

Smith, James K. A. 2009. *Desiring the Kingdom: Worship, Worldview, and Cultural Formation*. Grand Rapids, MI: Baker Academic.

Smith, James K. A. 2013. *Imagining the Kingdom: How Worship Works*. Grand Rapids, MI: Baker Academic. http://public.eblib.com/choice/publicfullrecord.aspx?p=3117117.

Smith, Stephen Decatur. 2010. "'We Look Away and Leap Around': Music, Ethics, and the Transcendental in Cavell and Adorno." *Journal of Music Theory* 54 (1): 121–140.

Smith, Wilfred Cantwell. 1979. *Faith and Belief: The Difference between Them*. Princeton, NJ: Princeton University Press.

Solomon, Lou. 2015. "Becoming Powerful Makes You Less Empathetic." *Harvard Business Review*, April 21, 2015. https://hbr.org/2015/04/becoming-powerful-makes-you-less-empathetic.

Spencer, Jon Michael. 1991. *Protest & Praise: Sacred Music of Black Religion*. Minneapolis, MN: Fortress Press.

Steuernagel, Marcell. 2018. "Church Music through the Lens of Performance: The Embodied Ritual of Sacred Play." Ph.D., United States -- Texas: Baylor University. http://search.proquest.com/docview/2099196278/abstract/A008EECB76AA4161PQ/1.

Stout, Jeffrey. 2001. *Ethics after Babel: The Languages of Morals and Their Discontents*. Princeton, NJ: Princeton University Press.

Stravinsky, Igor. 1998. *An Autobiography*. New York: W. W. Norton.

Stubbs, David L. 2004. "Liturgy and Ethics, or Liturgy Is Ethics." *Reformed Review* 57 (3): 1–12.

Suggate, Alan. 2002. "Worship and Ethics: Reflections on Conversations between Anglicans and Lutherans." *Studies in Christian Ethics* 15 (1): 54–65. https://doi.org/10.1177/095394680201500105.

Taylor, Angus. 2003. *Animals and Ethics: An Overview of the Philosophical Debate*. Tonawanda, NY: Broadview Press.

Taylor, Charles. 1992. *The Ethics of Authenticity*. Cambridge, MA: Harvard University Press.

Taylor, Charles. 2007. *A Secular Age*. Cambridge, MA: Belknap Press of Harvard University Press.

Terrien, Samuel L. 1952. *The Psalms and Their Meaning for Today*. 1st ed. Indianapolis, IN: Bobbs-Merrill.

Todt, Heinz Eduard. 2007. *Authentic Faith: Bonhoeffer's Theological Ethics in Context*. Grand Rapids, MI: W. B. Eerdmans.

Tong, Rosemarie. 2014. *Feminist Thought: A More Comprehensive Introduction*. 4th ed. Boulder, CO: Westview Press.

Townes, Emilie Maureen. 2006. *Womanist Ethics and the Cultural Production of Evil*. New York: Palgrave Macmillan.

Troeltsch, Ernst. 1960. *The Social Teaching of the Christian Churches*. Harper Torchbooks. Cloister Library 71–72. New York: Harper.

Tronto, Joan C. 1995. "Women and Caring: What Can Feminists Learn about Morality from Caring?" In *Justice and Care: Essential Readings in Feminist Ethics*, edited by Virginia Held, 101–116. Boulder, CO: Westview Press.

Trost, Wiebke, Sascha Frühholz, Daniele Schön, Carolina Labbé, Swann Pichon, Didier Grandjean, and Patrik Vuilleumier. 2014. "Getting the Beat: Entrainment of Brain Activity by Musical Rhythm and Pleasantness." *NeuroImage* 103: 55–64.

Turino, Thomas. 2008. *Music as Social Life: The Politics of Participation*. Chicago Studies in Ethnomusicology. Chicago: University of Chicago Press.

Ursu, Catalin. 2009. "Metamorphosis: A Pedagocial Phenomenology of Music, Ethics and Philosophy." PhD diss., Simon Fraser University (Canada). http://search.proquest.com/docview/1516260493/abstract/EC5BFEB4765A46E4PQ/1.

Vuilleumier, Patrik, and Wiebke Trost. 2015. "Music and Emotions: From Enchantment to Entrainment." *Annals of the New York Academy of Sciences* 1337 (March): 212–222. https://doi.org/10.1111/nyas.12676.

Wainwright, Geoffrey. 1984. *Doxology: A Systematic Theology*. Oxford University Press.

Waldman, Ellen. 2009. "Mindfulness, Emotions, and Ethics: The Right Stuff." *Nevada Law Journal* 10: 513.

Walker, Lorraine Olszewski, and Kay Coalson Avant. 2011. *Strategies for Theory Construction in Nursing*. 5th ed. Upper Saddle River, NJ: Pearson/Prentice Hall.

Wannenwetsch, Bernd. 2004. *Political Worship: Ethics for Christian Citizens*. Oxford Studies in Theological Ethics. Oxford University Press.

Ward, Pete, ed. 2012. *Perspectives on Ecclesiology and Ethnography*. Studies in Ecclesiology and Ethnography. Grand Rapids, MI: W. B. Eerdmans.

Warren, Jeff R. 2013. "Cobussen Marcel, Nanette Nielsen: Music and Ethics, Ashgate, 2012." *New Sound-International Magazine for Music*, no. 40–2: 229–232.

Warren, Jeff R. 2014. *Music and Ethical Responsibility*. New York: Cambridge University Press.

Warren, Jeff R. 2021. "'That Worship Sound': Ethics, Things, and Shimmer Reverberation." In *Ethics and Christian Musicking*, edited by Nathan Myrick and Mark Porter. Congregational Music Studies Series. New York: Routledge.

Webber, Robert E., and Lester Ruth. 2013. *Evangelicals on the Canterbury Trail: Why Evangelicals Are Attracted to the Liturgical Church*. Rev. ed. New York: Morehouse.

Westerfield-Tucker, Karen B. 2008. "'But Who Do You Say That I Am? Christology in Recent Protestant Hymnals." In *Place of Christ in Liturgical Prayer: Trinity, Christology, and Liturgical Theology*, edited by Bryan D. Spinks, 327–341. Collegeville, MN: Liturgical Press.

Westermeyer, Paul. 1997. *The Church Musician*. Rev. ed. Minneapolis, MN: Augsburg Fortress.

Westermeyer, Paul. 1998. *Let Justice Sing: Hymnody and Justice*. American Essays in Liturgy. Collegeville, MN: Liturgical Press.

Westermeyer, Paul. 2001. *The Heart of the Matter: Church Music as Praise, Prayer, Proclamation, Story and Gift*. Chicago: GIA.

Wheeler, Michael. 2017. "Martin Heidegger." In *The Stanford Encyclopedia of Philosophy*, edited by Edward N. Zalta, Fall 2017. Metaphysics Research Lab, Stanford University. https://plato.stanford.edu/archives/fall2017/entries/heidegger/.

Will, Udo, and Gabe Turow. 2011. "Introduction to Entrainment and Cognitive Ethnomusicology." In *Routledge Research in Music. Music, Science, and the Rhythmic Brain: Cultural and Clinical Implications*, edited by Jonathan Berger and Gabe Turow, 1–28. Florence, KY: Routledge.

Wilson, Fred. 2016. "John Stuart Mill." In *The Stanford Encyclopedia of Philosophy*, edited by Edward N. Zalta, Spring 2016. http://plato.stanford.edu/archives/spr2016/entries/mill/.

Wittgenstein, Ludwig. 2009. *Major Works*. Translated by C. K. Ogden. New York: HarperCollins.

Witvliet, John D. 2003. *Worship Seeking Understanding: Windows into Christian Practice*. Grand Rapids, MI: Baker Academic.

Wren, Brian A. 2000. *Praying Twice: The Music and Words of Congregational Song*. Louisville, KY: Westminster John Knox Press.

Wright, N. T. 2010. *After You Believe: Why Christian Character Matters*. New York: HarperOne.

Zehr, Howard. 1990. *Changing Lenses: A New Focus for Crime and Justice*. Palestine, TX: Herald Press.

Index

For the benefit of digital users, indexed terms that span two pages (e.g., 52–53) may, on occasion, appear on only one of those pages.

Figures are indicated by *f* following the page number